Death And Taxes

Hans F. Sennholz

Second Revised Edition

Center for Futures Education
1107 Washington Street
P. O. Box 489
Cedar Falls, Iowa 50613
(319) 277-7529

Library of Congress Catalog Card Number: 76-14537
International Standard Book Number 0-89195-017-6

Second revised edition published by
Center for Futures Education,
by arrangement with The Heritage Foundation

CONTENTS

Foreword   iv
1. On Private Property and Personal Wealth   1
2. On Taxation and Inflation   13
3. History of Federal Estate Taxes   28
4. Death Taxes as Equalizers   37
5. Effects on Predecessors   41
6. Effects on Successors   48
7. Avoidance and Evasion   56
8. Inflation Transfers Wealth — Tax Free   64
9. On Trusts and Trust Funds   70
10. Alternatives and Reform Proposals   77
Conclusion   100
Index   102

FOREWORD

Most people covet wealth, but how few understand its meaning! Few are aware that, in our private-property competitive order, wealth is productive capital consisting of means of production. It is assisting human labor in trade, commerce, industry, and agriculture, producing economic goods and services for consumers. To covet individual wealth and seize it by political force is to consume it, which renders human labor less efficient and less productive. It reduces wage rates and increases want and poverty.

In the coming years the protection of productive wealth will become increasingly difficult as inflation rages on and taxation becomes ever more onerous. Inflation and taxation will interact with the force of a vise whose jaws are squeezing prosperity and wealth out of our lives.

No government exaction is more destructive than a death duty that falls, almost exclusively, on productive capital. This monograph demonstrates that death duties cannot achieve the desired objective of economic equality, which lies beyond the power of any government no matter how much force it may apply. It seeks to demonstrate that the preservation of capital does not just serve family interest, but is a noble task that tends to benefit everyone. Knowledge of the financial complexities of death duties opens one of the few remaining avenues for the preservation of productive capital and family wealth. It is an avenue strewn with obstacles of law and regulation.

The monograph originally meant to make a contribution to the heated debate about death duties that transpired in 1975 and 1976 and led to important revisions in federal law. It was published by the Heritage Foundation as a study of public policy and its effects on American values.

This second edition is published by The Center for Futures Education in Cedar Falls, Iowa. Several new chapters have been added and the text updated to reflect the changes in U.S. tax laws.

I feel indebted to my colleagues for help and advice in the preparation of the book. In particular, I would like to express my gratitude to Professors Paul J. Fair, Charles J. Guiler, and our college librarian, Diane H. Grundy-McKillop. My gratitude is due to my son and his wife, Robert and Lyn, who urged me to prepare this edition. My heaviest debt is to my wife and partner of life.

Hans F. Sennholz

Grove City
September, 1982

Chapter 1
ON PRIVATE PROPERTY AND PERSONAL WEALTH

Death taxation probably has stimulated more philosophical, social and economic discussion among economists than any other type of taxation. Property transfers occasioned by death raise difficult questions on the nature and origin of property, and the rights to the property vacated by death. What are these rights and whence do they come? What do they seek to accomplish? As they are circumscribed by present laws are they most suited to serve the best interests of society? And what are these interests? Such questions are submitted to the test of free discussion whenever the right of inheritance comes under review.

Throughout the history of man, private property has resulted from acquisition of ownerless things, from violent expropriation of previous owners, or from production by human skill and energy. When William the Conquerer subdued England he redistributed the land simultaneously with the conquest of the country. At every stage of the conquest his Norman followers received new rewards. Almost every English landholder of importance was dispossessed, including those who had not borne arms against him. William thus created vast fiefs subject to feudal obligations as the foundation of his rule and power. Transfer of land, both from the dead to the living, and from the living to the living, was the sovereign right of the conquerer. He could refuse to grant investiture of an estate to another member of the family, and instead bestow it on any other vassal. Or he could choose to keep it himself. But when he consented to a transfer, the heir and new vassal paid a duty, generally a year's rent, which throughout the Middle Ages constituted a principal source of revenue for the crown.

There are few American families today whose title to land goes back directly to original grants by the kings of England, France, or Spain. Private property generally comes into existence through production of a myriad of man-made goods, or through exchange of such goods for the nature-given factor, which is land. The history of property no longer traces the records of conquest, but consults the ledgers

1

of exchange or production. Surely, some American land now privately owned can be traced back to violent expropriation from native Indians. They in turn had expropriated it from other Indians, who in the past had appropriated it upon their arrival. But today's ownership in land is no longer linked with this remote origin of property. It resulted from economic exchanges freely entered upon by individuals and was paid in full with man-made goods or labor services.

In primitive history, private property as an aggregate of rights which are guaranteed and protected by the government, had its origin with government. William the Conqueror was the creator and dispenser of property rights. All the land in England was his gift. In a peaceful society that lives on production and exchange, property rights come into existence through the production and exchange of economic goods with exchangeable value, which makes up wealth or estate. Government no longer is the creator of property; it is merely the protector of valuable rights and interests. The process of production that creates wealth, which is the subject of property, simultaneously brings into being the property rights over this wealth. The members of rich nations enjoy high standards of living because they are highly productive nations that every day are creating more income, wealth, and property. Poor countries, whose people suffer from hunger and want, are comparatively unproductive. They, too, occupy fertile land and natural resources, but without employment of much productive wealth, human labor is rather ineffective. Severe restrictions on private property, which are so popular in poor countries, may have a direct bearing on the quantity of income and wealth that is created.

Property rights created by force and expropriation must be defended continually by force lest the producers attempt to retrieve their losses. For five years William the Conqueror met with rebellions, which he managed to crush by ravaging and devastating the country. This system of property built on force has existed throughout the ages, and lives on in contemporary command systems of social organization, whether they are communist, fascist or socialist. Whenever they have come to power, these governments have seized the means of production and substituted government control for private ownership. Government then manages the production process and determines the distribution and allocation of the yield. Private property is forcibly limited to consumer goods, which government allocates and dispenses.

In an exchange economy, commonly called the market system or capitalism, private ownership of the means of production is a fundamental institution. It springs from production and comes into existence peacefully. It, too, needs to be defended from those who would violate it. But in contrast to the command system that must forever be on guard against the countless victims of its order, the property that springs from peaceful effort and voluntary exchange needs to be protected merely from a few criminals who steal and plunder, or love to inflict harm on their fellowmen.

In the private property order and voluntary exchange system, private ownership means full control over the uses and services of property, not merely a legal title while government is holding the power of control. The proprietor alone determines the employment of his productive wealth. But to enjoy any advantages of this wealth, it must be employed in the service of consumers. Productive wealth is submitted to the wishes of the public. The people, through their buying or abstention from buying, determine not only individual income but also capital ownership. Private ownership thus becomes a *production function*.

Private property is no special privilege enjoyed by the owner class. It is a natural institution that facilitates orderly production and division of labor. Private ownership of the means of production is in the interest of everyone, for it assures the most economic employment of scarce resources. The efficient entrepreneur, who produces what the people want in the most efficient manner, acquires control over productive capital. His wealth mainly consists of capital employed in the production of goods for the people.

The critics of capitalism who deplore the differences in personal wealth overlook this characteristic of productive wealth. A millionaire's fortune does not consist of idle luxuries, but of factories, machines, and equipment that produce for the people, give employment, and yield wages. The successful entrepreneur usually does enjoy a higher standard of living than his employees. The car he drives may be a later model. The suit he wears may be custom-made, and his

3

house may have wall-to-wall carpeting. But his living conditions do not differ essentially from those of his workers. The businessman's power is derived from the sovereign power of consumers. His ability to manage wisely the factors of production earns him the consumers' support. It is not anchored in legal privilege, custom, or tradition, but in his ability to serve the only sovereign boss of the capitalist economy: the consumer. The businessman, no matter how great his wealth and power may appear, must cater to the whims and wishes of the buyers. To neglect them spells disaster to him. Henry Ford rose to fame and fortune when he produced millions of cars that people liked and wanted. But during the late 1920's their tastes and preferences began to change. They sought a greater variety of bigger and better cars which Ford refused to manufacture. Consequently, while other companies, such as General Motors and Chrysler, grew by leaps and bounds, the Ford enterprise suffered staggering losses. The power and reputation of Henry Ford declined, for a time, as rapidly as it had grown during the earlier decades.

An individual enterprise society is a haven for workingmen, who are the great beneficiaries of its order. One merely needs to compare the working and living conditions of the American worker with those of his counterparts in noncapitalistic countries, such as India or Communist China. He is the prince among the world's laborers; his work week is the shortest; his physical exertion the least; and his wages are by far the highest.

The millionaire is less enviable in capitalism than in noncapitalist societies. His wealth mainly consists of capital investments, which he must continually manage in competition with other businessmen. His consumptive wealth, usually a minor fraction of his total wealth, may be rather modest. But the Indian millionaire, most likely a rajah, is not concerned with production and competition. He resides in an exotic mansion with a treasure chest of jewels and precious metals, surrounded and catered to by dozens of eager servants. He does not envy the American businessman, however great his wealth may be.

Business Profits

In a market system great personal wealth may flow from business profits. Therefore, many critics are disturbed about "obscene profits" which some businessmen are said to be reaping. Since profits are unpredictable returns of business, ranging from a mere fraction of one percent to many times the capital invested, these critics voice their suspicion of manipulated irregularities, of unfair advantages, and unethical practices. They often conclude that great profits are "unearned incomes" extracted from the low wages of workers or gouged from consumers through high prices. This is why business profits should be taxed severely when they accrue, and again when they appear as great wealth in a businessman's estate.

Economists who analyze the economic nature of "profits" perceive three distinct sources of income. Most proprietors and partners of small businesses who think they are reaping "profits" actually earn what economists call *managerial remuneration*. They are earning an income through their own managerial labor, supervising their employees, serving customers, working with salesmen, accountants, and auditors. Obviously, their services are very valuable in the labor market. They would earn a good salary if they were to work for the A & P or a 5 & 10¢ store. Therefore, that part of a businessman's income which is earned through his own labor is a kind of wage or salary, and as such, is totally unrelated to economic profits.

But the majority of American enterprises earn an income in excess of managerial remuneration. The economist who dissects this residuum finds two other parts. By far the largest part, which is earned by the majority of American enterprises, is *interest* on the owner's or stockholder's invested capital. It accrues to the owner on account of the time-consuming nature of the production process. Whoever refrains from spending his income and wealth and, instead, invests them in time-consuming production can expect a return. For without such a return no one would relinquish his savings to provide capital for production. Interest ultimately flows from human nature. Men of all ages and races value their present cash more highly than a claim payable in the future. In order to induce an investor to relinquish his cash for production, which will yield its fruits in the future, a premium called *originary interest*, must be paid. In other words, the businessman who invests in his own enterprise hopes to earn the same kind of income on his investment as the lender who extends a loan to a borrower.

Finally, there are enterprises that do earn *pure profits*. Through correct anticipation of future economic conditions, businessmen may earn what economists call entrepreneurial profits. For instance, by purchasing when prices are low and selling when prices are higher, they may earn inventory profits. After interest allowance is made for the time of investment, stock market profits are pure profits. Of course, such profits are connected with risk because of the uncertainty of the future. Instead of reaping profits, many businessmen suffer losses.

Contrary to popular belief, pure profits are short-lived. Whenever a change in demand, supply, fashion or technology opens up an opportunity for pure profits, the early producer reaps high returns. Immediately he will be imitated by competitors and newcomers. They will produce the same goods, render identical services, apply similar methods of production and thus depress prices until the pure profit disappears. The first transistor manufacturer undoubtedly reaped pure profits. But as soon as competitors had retooled their factories, the market was flooded with transistors. Prices dropped rapidly until the pure profits had vanished. When the American people suddenly discovered their need for compact cars, American Motors, which was the early manufacturer, temporarily earned pure profits. After General Motors, Chrysler and Ford invaded the field, American Motors' profits returned to the market rate of interest and even changed to losses.

Pure profits are very elusive. But opportunities for profits will emerge as long as there are changes in demand, supply, fashion, population, technology or even the weather. As all life is change, and economic adjustments need to be made continuously, opportunities for profits will arise again and again. Taxation of pure profits or their distribution to workers would eliminate the incentive for risk-taking and hurt workers in the long run. Why should a man risk his capital in production if he can only suffer losses or merely earn five percent interest? In that case he would shun productive investment, and search for riskless employment of his funds. The economy would thus become rigid and inflexible and unable to adjust to changes in demand, supply and technology. Expansion and modernization would be severely hampered.

Professional Incomes

Great personal wealth may also flow from professional fees and executive salaries. The plastic surgeon who knows how to rejuvenate the facial features of aging ladies may earn honoraria that greatly exceed the wages of teachers and plumbers. His skill may be so rare and his reputation so great that patients flock to him from distant places, seeking his service. To elderly ladies, his operation that restores their appearance of youth through a skillful face-lifting, may be worth more than a small number in a savings account book or a few shares of G.M. common stock. Thus, the surgeon may prosper and acquire personal wealth.

Executive salaries and bonuses may amount to hundreds of thousands of dollars per year. People unfamiliar with the principles that determine wage and salary rates are apt to become envious and receptive to ideas that are hostile to great personal wealth.

The selection of corporate management confronts stockholders with choices similar to those we all face in our daily purchase decisions. Should they look for management at bargain rates? Should they shop for medium-priced management, or search for the best possible men who demand top salaries? As in everyday life, the best is often the cheapest in the long run. The stockholder must hire the men who do the actual work for him. He is aware that the mistakes of corporate executives can consume a large percentage of net income or even eliminate it altogether, yet the right men may earn large profits and greatly enhance the value of the corporation. Depending on the size of the business, the selection of management may mean a difference of millions of dollars in profits or losses.

In the history of the automobile industry the stockholders of dozens of independent companies had this choice to make. Many of them chose management at bargain rates — and lost their investments when the companies fell by the wayside. The managerial salaries in those cases, no matter how low, proved to be no bargains. At the same time, the obscure and failing Maxwell-Chalmers Corporation hired Walter P. Chrysler, who built it into one of the big three of the industry. His compensation, no matter how high, constituted a real bargain to the corporate owners. The workers also gain from superior management. Contrary to popular notions, the workers' interests are served best under superior management. Wages tend to be higher in a profitable and expanding exterprise than in a failing one. Fringe benefits are higher and jobs more secure. Rejoicing about cheap management can be very shortsighted — and short-lived.

In bidding for managerial services in the executive labor market, each corporation is in competition not only with all other corporations, but also with the opportunities for the manager to organize a business of his own. This competition is reflected in salaries, as well as in pensions, bonuses, and other benefits. And the calculations are in terms of *net* salaries and *net* benefits after taxes.

Competition largely determines how much the corporation has to pay for a good manager. When an executive is hired, his future contribution can merely be estimated. Economic prudence therefore requires that he be paid merely the amount that induces him to accept employment. This minimum is determined by competition in the executive labor market. Once he proves to be a capable entrepreneur who adds profits to the company, his remuneration tends to go up. The corporation now must increase his remuneration, lest he accept employment with a competitor who also recognizes his ability to create profits. To avoid paying ever higher executive salaries, many companies resort to less costly forms of remuneration. For instance, they may grant purchase options that give executives the right to buy from the company a certain number of shares of stock at prices lower than the market price. Besides the savings in costs, this method has an additional attraction. The executive becomes co-owner, giving him new incentives for doing his utmost in the service of the company.

Executive salaries and wealth ultimately are determined and paid by the consumers. Through buying or abstention from buying, consumers determine which corporations are to earn profits or suffer losses. They determine the remuneration of Frank Sinatra, Elizabeth Taylor and Muhammad Ali. They also determine and pay the workers' wages as well as the executive salaries at General Motors and U.S. Steel.

But high individual productivity alone never creates personal wealth. Famous athletes, entertainers, and executives may enjoy impressive incomes. Yet, if they are lacking the most essential ingredient of wealth formation, the habit of thrift and concern for the future, their economic existence may be as insecure and precarious as that of a pauper.

In Search of Equality

Many critics of our economic and social order point at a chasm that divides the class of underprivileged, poverty-stricken Americans from the class of the privileged wealthy and rich. The United States, they charge, is the richest and most powerful country the world has known, yet poverty and inequality continue to characterize the American system and remain crucial domestic problems. Violence, racial conflict, and decaying cities are symptoms of dehumanizing poverty which American society has failed to eradicate. The "system of privilege" under capitalism is the principal cause of this poverty, as "privileged" income creates concentrations of wealth and disparities of income. Therefore, the income earned and received by the privileged groups of society must be redistributed to the poor, the aged, the handicapped, the sick, and the unemployed. Government, as the agent of society, must address itself to the reduction of the incomes and wealth of the privileged rich, and especially the diminution of family wealth that is passed intact from one generation to the next.

Such are the hopes and aspirations of large segments of the American population. The political parties and pressure groups are reflecting this public opinion, engaging in policies designed to eradicate poverty and reduce inequality. Since the 1930's, the political intent of both parties has been this very program. We have seen the introduction of progressive income taxes that took as much as 94 percent of top personal incomes, after business taxes claimed as much as 90 percent of excess profits. We have seen the imposition of federal estate levies that confiscated as much as 77 percent of large estates. Yet, the concentrations of large fortunes and incomes have continued to the dismay and frustration of the social reformers.

As economists we must not judge those hopes and aspirations. If eradication of poverty and reduction of inequality are the objectives of the majority of society, we would expect government, as the agent of the majority, to pass laws and regulations to realize these objectives. After all, public opinion tends to shape the general course of policy. But it is the very function of economists to deliberate on the suitable methods and policies that are capable of achieving the given objectives. Economists can recommend the means most appropriate for the attainment of given goals. That is, they can recommend the policies that are most suited to eradicate poverty and reduce inequality. If government should resort to policies that are ineffective, or even make things worse, economists must not hesitate to oppose such policies and point at their inevitable consequences. This is their function and service to society.

Only this vantage point of the economist allows a scientific discussion of the problems of poverty and inequality. It raises and answers the questions whether these objectives can be achieved, whether the proposed policies and programs are suited to achieve them, and, if found unsuitable, what their inevitable consequences must be. Any other analysis is rather fruitless when conducted from the points of view of aesthetics, ethics, anthropology, psychology, sociology, or politics. Emotional descriptions of individual cases of poverty or wealth may arouse apprehension and agitation, and even political reaction, but they are incapable of solving the problems. In fact, they frequently invite application of hasty, unsuitable means which in the end make matters worse.

Any intelligent discussion of poverty and its remedies must begin with a clear definition of the problem we seek to solve. What is poverty? The answer to this basic question may be given in relative as well as absolute terms.

Most contemporatry critics of poverty refer to the living conditions of the lowest fifth, fourth, or third of the American population. President Franklin D. Roosevelt in his Second Inaugural Address in January, 1937, saw "one-third of a nation ill-housed, ill-clad, ill-nourished." President Johnson when he was launching his "war on poverty," in January, 1964, observed that "one-fifth of our families and nearly one-fifth of our total population are poor." It should be obvious that this use of the term makes the problem forever insoluble. No matter how productive and affluent a society should be, there would always be the lowest third, fourth, or fifth that is poorer than all others — unless there is total uniformity of living conditions. Such a state of complete equality surpasses our human understanding; it presumes a ruthless equalizing force that in itself denies every pretense of equality.

When poverty is described in absolute terms we are stymied by such value judgments as "decent standard of living" or "ability to satisfy minimum needs." What is the standard of decency? And what are these minimum needs? How can so many millions of Americans exist year after year, surviving below the level of minimum needs? The absolute term of poverty thus becomes a relative term that can be shifted in accordance with the political objective to be served by the definition. To alleviate relative poverty is to redistribute income and wealth until every member of society enjoys precisely the same economic amenities. Any measure short of this goal would preserve a difference, and necessitate further redistribution.[1]

Let us assume that government, as the executor of forced redistribution, consists of just and honest men who can be entrusted with the equalization program. Let us further assume that politicians will not enrich themselves or their constituents. Even with these assumptions, the objective is unrealizable. Income and wealth constitute no given stream of worldly goods provided by the inexorable laws of nature. They are created every day through individual effort and initiative. To seize income and wealth from their producers must reduce production and output. Man strives and labors purposely to achieve certain results. If the results are denied him by force, he cannot be expected to labor. Furthermore, the beneficiaries of redistribution may relax in their efforts to contribute to the production process. Therefore, forced redistribution inevitably reduces the stream of goods and thus intensifies the problem of poverty. As the stream narrows because of continuous seizures and transfers, it may finally shrink to a brook that can no longer support the millions of people whose lives depend on it. If carried to its final conclusion, forced redistribution jeopardizes man's existence.

Although economic equality can never be fully achieved, many may continue to seek it on a limited scale. However,

---

[1]For an excellent analysis of poverty cf. Henry Hazlitt, *The Conquest of Poverty*. New Rochelle, N.Y.: Arlington House, 1973; also Rose D. Friedman, Poverty: *Definition and Perspective*. Washington, D.C.: American Enterprise Institute, 1965.

all such efforts reduce economic output which, in the long run, may deprive the poorer people of more income than the redistribution may give them. For most needy Americans this point has long been passed after more than fifty years of transfer policy. In fiscal 1983, the federal government alone is scheduled to spend $261.7 billion on "income security." (*The Budget* for 1983, p. 3-34). If this amount were invested productively, the standards of living of all Americans, including the least productive, would rise substantially. After some 50 years, the transfer system has consumed incalculable amounts of productive capital that could be paying wages far in excess of today's transfer payments.

Chapter 2
ON TAXATION AND INFLATION

Taxes are compulsory exactions of private income and wealth for governmental purposes. Throughout most of human history they were the mark of bondage — of slaves, vassals, colonists, and conquered peoples supporting their rulers. They were the revenue exacted by the state primarily for the support of the favored few, the king and his court.

During the 19th and 20th centuries popular governments shifted the burdens and benefits, but did not materially change their nature. Taxation gradually became an exaction of ever increasing proportions of "national income" for the support of popular policies. Taxes became the sinews of popular wars to eradicate slavery or bring peace and democracy to the world. In moments of peace, taxation was redirected toward social and political objectives. Vocal pressure groups yielding great political power through their chosen representatives now demand services and benefits at the expense of other groups. But in contrast to the distant past when powerful minorities exacted income and wealth from their numerous subjects, the popular majorities now seize their benefits from politically weaker minorities, in particular, from people with higher incomes.

The Constitution of the United States, which is a monument to individual liberty, did not envision such taxation. Drafted and ratified when political and economic freedom were uppermost in the minds of the people, the Constitution sanctioned the levying of import duties while it prohibited export duties. "Direct taxes" when used by the federal government were to be apportioned among the states according to their respective population numbers. This provision ruled out not only federal property taxation but also income levies because they could not be apportioned among the states according to their numbers. In response to public demands for more federal services and benefits, the Sixteenth Amendment to the Constitution, adopted in 1913, finally opened the gates by permitting the Congress to enact laws taxing income and wealth from whatever source without regard to apportionment.

Wars Beget Taxes

Taxes must increase when government expenditures grow. Within certain limits expenditures may be met temporarily by borrowing the needed funds; but eventually the revenues must keep up with outlays. The reasons for the growth of taxation, therefore, are the very reasons for the increase in government expenditures. James Madison, fourth President of the United States, pointed at the most important cause for great increases in government expenditures and taxes: "Of all the evils to public liberty, *war* is perhaps the most to be dreaded, because it comprises and develops every other. War is the parent of armies; from these proceed debts and taxes. And armies, and debts, and taxes, are the known instruments for bringing the many under the dominion of the few."

The three major wars in U.S. history clearly illustrate his point. In the prosecution of the Civil war, federal government expenditures rose nearly twentyfold, from $66.5 million in fiscal year 1861 to $1.2976 billion in 1865. In World War I, federal expenditures soared more than twenty-six times, from $724 million in 1916 to $18.952 billion in 1919. In World War II, they increased nearly tenfold, from $9.456 billion in 1940 to $92.69 billion in 1945. In just a few years of hostility every tax which man could conceive was levied and raised, every subject was brought under the tax system. After the wars the expenditures, while declining at first, remained far above the prewar levels, servicing the swollen federal debt and compensating victims and veterans.

As never before, the essence of nuclear war is fire, famine and pestilence. Federal expenditures and taxes, which now (1982) exceed $725 billion per year, would rise at least ten to twentyfold, and seize every penny of visible income and wealth. It is difficult to imagine how, under such conditions, man can survive the compulsory exactions even if he should survive the nuclear holocaust. Ultimately, his civilization may give way to a state of hopeless barbarism.

Business Depressions Raise Government Expenditures and Taxes

Government expenditures multiply and taxes rise in periods of economic emergency. Popular explanations of depressions lay the blame on the private enterprise system and expect relief and recovery from an expanding scope of

14

governmental functions. The Great Depression beginning in 1930 caused government expenditures, particularly on the federal level, to rise markedly over the preceding period. In 1929, the federal government spent $3.127 billion; in 1940, it spent $9.456 billion, or three times the pre-depression outlay. The funds were obtained largely by means of deficit financing; but taxes were rising steadily relative to individual incomes.

Economic activity in our age of central banking and government control over money and banking is subject to frequent cyclical changes. Periods of feverish boom are followed by periods of painful stagnation and depression, which are followed by new booms and depressions. During the depression phase government is expected to embark upon contracyclical spending in order to offset the lack of spending of the other sectors. It is expected to tax away idle purchasing-power hoards and create new spending power through currency and credit expansion. When the stagnation finally gives way to feverish activity and rising prices, government once again is expected to raise taxes in order to take away the excess purchasing power. The expenditure and tax arguments are changing throughout the cycle, but the net effect remains the same: the scope of governmental functions is expanding and taxes are rising.

From the 1930's to the 1980's the economic objective that guided most tax decisions has been the cure of depression and inflation. Under the influence of Keynesian economic thought, taxes are raised or lowered, surtaxes are imposed or repealed, tax credits for equipment purchases are granted or repealed, in a never-ending political play of "tax reform" in order to manage the cyclical movements of the economy. Unfortunately, such policies neither fight inflation nor alleviate unemployment. During the 1970's they gave us both double-digit inflation and exceptionally high unemployment.

Inflation, which is the creation of money and credit by monetary authorities (the Federal Reserve System and the U.S. Treasury), cannot be neutralized, nullified or offset by tax increases. One billion dollars of new money injected into the banking system constitutes a net addition to the stock of money even if the Treasury should seize a similar amount from millions of taxpayers. It would bring forth inflationary effects even if the new money were granted directly to the Treasury. In fact, tax increases on business income and productive capital tend to reduce business activity and economic output, which in turn tends to raise goods prices. Tax boosts seriously aggravate the inflation; they do not alleviate it.

Financing Public Services

Since the 1930's, especially, public expenditures have risen in reaction to popular demand for government services which, necessarily, were accompanied by increases in taxes. Such increases may be less spectacular than those for wars and depressions, but they nonetheless, in recent years, have become a crushing burden that is eroding our economic substance and destroying our social order.

Although an effort was recently made to strengthen U.S. military posture through additional defense spending, only 29¢ of the 1983 federal budget dollar are allocated to defense. 43¢ are disbursed as direct benefit payments to individuals, 11¢ as grants to state and localities, and 13¢ as net interest on the federal debt.[2] 28% of all federal spending is going to elderly Americans. Through Medicaid and Medicare, the federal government is paying for the medical care of approximately 47 million Americans, or some 20% of our total population and 99% of those over 65. The federal government is subsidizing approximately 95 million meals per day, or 14% of all meals served in the United States. It is offering 6.9 million post-secondary awards or loans to students, benefiting nearly everyone who cares to apply.[3] In short, it is engaged in the most massive redistribution of income and wealth ever attempted in modern times.

The most ominous aspect of these federal services must not be sought in their soaring costs and tax burdens on the working population. It is the "redistributive" aspect of all government services that is giving cause to alarm. Government has no source of independent income and wealth of its own. Every penny it spends must first be taken from someone who produced it. Every dollar it spends on social service must be taken from a producer of income. It enriches the

---

[2]Budget of the U.S. Government, Fiscal Year, 1983, p. M2.
[3]Executive Office of the President, Office of Management and Budget, Press Release, March 12, 1982.

16

beneficiaries while it impoverishes taxpayers. The beneficiaries are not bidding for the service in an open market, willing to pay the market price. They are clamoring for it on the political scene where someone else will be forced to cover the costs.

"Public service" means vociferous redistribution of individual income and wealth by political force, which is divisive socially and politically, and destructive economically. It creates insoluble social conflict between the beneficiaries who create their entitlements by majority vote, and the victims who are forced to surrender individual income and wealth. It reflects a dangerous state of political immorality that is gnawing at the very foundation of society.

The political immorality that has infected all groups and classes of society is fostered and nourished by some strange notions of humanitarianism. People who in their personal lives would never harm others are quite willing to seize other people's income and wealth through the political process. They favor public expenditure and taxation for health, old age pension, higher education, and countless other political services. Unfortunately, they fail to perceive the crucial difference between private charity, which is a laudable act of benevolence, good will, or affection reflecting the love of man for his fellowman, and political redistribution, which is force and coercion breeding social conflict and government power.

To Equalize Incomes

Our present tax structure openly aims at greater equalization of income and wealth through tax rate progression. However, this does not mean that the system relieves the lowest income brackets from a proportional share of the tax burden. On the contrary, it has been proven by a number of able economists that even the poorest people pay a higher percentage of their income in indirect taxes than does the class with the greatest number of taxpayers.

F. A. Hayek,[4] eminent Austrian economist and Nobel Prize laureate, found that it was not the poorest, but the most numerous, and therefore politically most powerful, classes which were taxed relatively lightly, while not only

---

[4] F. A. Hayek, *The Constitution of Liberty*, The University of Chicago Press, 1960, pp. 312, 313.

17

those above them, but also those below them, were burdened more heavily — approximately in proportion to their smaller political strength.

Taxation is no simple government matter. It presents problems of shifting, diffusion, and incidence — difficulties that challenge even the ablest economist. Every tax sets into operation a chain of reactions that affect industrial production, wages, income, employment, standard of living, mode of living, and so on. Most legislators probably are unaware of the numerous economic effects of the taxes imposed.

They may be unaware that the steep graduation of the income tax accomplishes the very opposite of what it was meant to do. It perpetuates economic and social inequalities and thereby creates a rigid class structure that divides society. The expropriation of high incomes effectively prevents formation of capital and wealth that facilitates individual improvement. How can an able newcomer from the wrong side of town rise in economic and social position if his "excess income" is expropriated at every turn of success? How can he challenge the business establishment, with its hereditary wealth and position, if he is prevented from accumulating the necessary capital?

On the other hand, old businesses can relax. They can become inefficient and bureaucratic, because newcomers with "excess profits" are prevented by confiscatory taxation from challenging the establishment. The tax progression does prevent the rich from growing richer; but it also protects them from competition by ambitious and able newcomers. Thus the rich stay rich, and the poor stay poor. This gives birth to economic and social classes. Instead of individual effort and productivity, the coincidence of birth and inheritance becomes the main economic determinant for most individuals.

To Equalize Wealth

These are undesirable economic and social conditions. To alleviate them, government must choose between removing the causes that brought them about or engaging in further intervention in an attempt to cope with the consequences of prior intervention. Removing the causes by reducing the tax progression would be difficult, as it implies an admission of failure. Public opinion once favored the progression and

18

therefore may be slow in comprehending the failure and approving the necessary change in policy. As a consequence, we must expect government to opt for the alternative: to resort to further intervention on grounds that earlier policies were not comprehensive enough.

Many reform proposals on federal estate and gift taxation must be seen in this light. Previous policies aimed at economic and social equality not only have failed in their professed objectives, but actually have contributed to economic stagnation and inequality. If business levies and individual income taxes did not achieve the desired equality, a direct attack on personal property may be more effective. And if the early rates do not succeed, they can be raised again, and "loopholes" can be closed, until all traces of inequality have been eradicated. Such is the rationale of the equalization program.

Many laws and regulations are concerned with economic and social equality, which to contemporary society is a major *moral* objective. They are moral laws that are to reform society. Surely, tax legislation that seeks to collect needed revenue for changing or stabilizing the economy, to equalize incomes or wealth, represents a system of morality. A 77 percent estate tax levied on widows and orphans presupposes a strong moral system that aims at remaking society.

Earlier generations of Americans sought justice and order under law. They pursued the ideal that everyone was equal under the law, whose only function was the restraint of evildoers. They expected little from government, which was merely man's agency of such restraint. The new America that took shape in our century is a reformatory for man and society. Government has become a powerful agency of reform and redistribution that serves to alleviate poverty, inequality, ignorance, and anything else considered to be evil. And tax laws are its potent instruments.

The history of federal estate taxation offers a perfect example of this transformation and its inevitable consequences. When the function of law and state was limited to punishing and restraining evil-doers, there was no place for progressive death duties. A 77 percent capital levy on wealthy families would have been inconceivable to our forebears. They rose in rebellion with much less provocation than that. But their descendants, who converted to a new, earnestly humanistic faith and morality,[5] not only imposed such a levy, but are coverting ever more. The beautiful ideal of equality under the law has given way to the new ideal of economic equality by force.

The desired objective of economic equality lies beyond the power of any government to achieve, and tax levies designed to equalize income and wealth not only are ineffective, but also harmful to peace and order. Federal estate taxation, no matter how steeply graduated, not only is an ineffective source of revenue but also aggravates the economic inequality it is supposed to alleviate. This conclusion, elaborated in Chapter IV, points up a basic economic law or principle: *Economic and social inequality is inversely related to economic productivity, income and wealth.* Inequality tends to grow with declining labor productivity; it tends to diminish with rising labor productivity. A progressive estate tax that seizes and consumes productive capital, therefore, is a powerful instrument for inequality.

Although the tax act of 1981 provided for a gradual reduction of the maximum rate of estate taxation to 50 percent, the tax itself continues to be one of the most destructive exactions ever devised. It plays havoc with productive capital that provides jobs and incomes to the working population. It forces highly productive individuals to redirect their efforts toward less productive pursuits, or may compel them to create wealth that is less visible to estate tax collectors. It may induce them to join the rapidly growing "underground economy" where personal wealth takes the form of jewelry, precious metals, art objects, collectors' items, etc. They may shift their liquid capital to safer shores abroad and accumulate income and wealth in foreign places. Or, they may just cease to be productive and openly embark upon consumption of their accumulated wealth. Their reaction may explain the rapid growth of the luxury industries that cater to ostentatious consumption, while many essential industries are gradually sinking in poverty and despair.

In conjunction with rampant inflation the estate tax is gradually destroying all the visible wealth of a country. Inflation is slowly lifting all taxable estates into a maximum

---

[5]R. J. Rushdoony, *Law and Liberty,* Nutley, N.J.: The Craig Press, 1971, p. 4; also his *Politics of Guilt and Pity,* the Craig Press, 1970, p. 97 *et seq.*

tax bracket where they await seizure and consumption by government. If inflation is destined to destroy the American dollar later in this century, which is the dire forecast of so many capable economists, the estate tax will add its destruction to the poverty and chaos that will descend over the country.

Inflation

Inflation is sometimes described as a tax on the money holders. In reality, it is a terrible instrument for the redistribution of wealth. Government undoubtedly is its greatest profiteer as tax revenues are boosted by the built-in progression of income and death duties, and government debt is depreciated. Inflation also shifts wealth from those classes of society who are unable, or do not know how, to defend themselves from the monetary destruction, to entrepreneurs and owners of material means of production. It strengthens the position of some businessmen, while it lowers the real wages of most working men and professionals. It decimates or destroys altogether the middle class of investors, who own securities or hold claims to life insurance and pension payments. Finally, it gives birth to a new class of traders, speculators, and profiteers of the monetary depreciation.

The redistribution process is also a massive debt liquidation process in real terms. The nominal magnitude of dollar debt is rising, but in terms of real things and real values, debt is being liquidated at the depreciation rate. A ten percent rate of currency depreciation reduces real debt by ten percent; total monetary destruction destroys debt totally. It transfers the ownership of real wealth from the people who have lent money to the people who have borrowed the money.

In general, the middle class generates the financial capital that affords productivity and expansion to commerce and industry. It holds a large share of national wealth in the form of financial capital, such as corporate stock and debentures, demand and time deposits, life insurance, pension funds, etc. All of these suffer serious losses from the depreciation of the currency. In fact, rampant inflation expropriates the wealth and substance of this middle class.

The depreciation of public debt and the fall of industrial securities in terms of both price and purchasing power strike

21

a devastating blow not only at millions of small investors but also at great capitalists whose wealth is invested in monetary claims and securities. Wealthy stock brokers, bankers, financiers, *rentiers*, heirs, or businessmen in retirement, who before the inflation owned large fortunes, suffer serious losses. Old fortunes vanish, and eminent family names fade away. Similarly, the wealth of charitable institutions, religious societies, scientific or literary foundations, and endowed colleges and universities is destroyed by inflation.

When money incomes rise because of inflation, everyone is lifted into progressively higher income brackets. Inflation, together with the feature of tax progression, allows the government to absorb an ever-larger share of the people's earnings. In short, inflation pushes us all towards the top rate of income taxation.

Business income and taxation are especially affected by monetary depreciation. When prices rise, a distortion of profits takes place. They are made to appear far larger than they actually are. Inflation drives the costs of replacing plant and equipment far above the original cost. But for tax purposes, the government recognizes only the original cost, thus forcing business to overstate actual earnings. It levies income taxes on imaginary profits that, in reality, are inflationary costs of replacement.[6]

The same is true with estate taxation. As inflation gradually raises the value of every estate beyond the basic exemption, government is absorbing an ever larger share of estates. In fact, inflation and tax progression are pushing all estates towards the top rate of taxation. It is even conceivable that hyperinflation, together with progressive tax duties, may permit government to expropriate and nationalize most facilities of production within one generation.

When inflation raises prices, personal wealth appears far larger than it actually is. The small farmer on a five-hundred-acre spread is suddenly elevated to a country squire, whose wealth in depreciated dollars becomes the

---

[6]H. F. Sennholz, "Two-Digit Inflation," *The Freeman*, Irvington-on-Hudson, N.Y.: The Foundation for Economic Education, Inc., January 1975, p. 23 *et seq.*

tion are boosting goods prices in accordance with the "law of cost." But also those taxes levied primarily on consumption, such as the income taxes paid by workers, make their way into prices. The $4,000 income tax withheld from the steel worker's annual pay is a real cost to the steel mill like the wages paid directly to the worker. As such, the very amount of tax withheld is reflected in steel prices. A boost in his income tax reduces the worker's take-home pay; it does not reduce the steel production costs; therefore, it does not lower steel prices. A boost of those labor taxes which directly raise production costs — such as payroll taxes, employment taxes, and Social Security taxes — does affect profit margins. Consequently this increase affects output, supply, and ultimately prices.

The price of an automobile thus embodies all its costs of material, capital, and labor, including all income taxes withheld from the paychecks of everyone participating in its production, from the chairman of the board to the night janitor, and all business taxes levied directly upon its production. A steelworker who finally purchases the automobile must cover all these costs in the purchase price. Ironically the costs include his own income taxes withheld from his paycheck when he produced the steel for the car. In short, his income taxes reduce his take-home pay. With his take-home pay thus reduced he can buy the product at a price including his total labor costs *and* including his own income taxes. He pays income taxes and then pays for them in the price of the product.

The Nouveaux Riches

Huge private fortunes and imposing concentrations of capital are formed from inflationary redistribution. But in contrast to the formation of capital under stable monetary conditions, when fortunes are built through productive changes and improvements, through technological inventions and efficient methods of production, the wealth derived from inflation may be "redistributive," from one individual to another. The new millionaires are not generally creators of new industries or reorganizers of production. They are mostly clever speculators with excellent understanding of monetary policy and its effects on stock prices, exchange rates and high finance. They may even be industrialists who are turning away from the hard work of business management to the more rewarding dealings in securities, commodities, and foreign exchange. But above all, they understand the phenomenon of inflation and use this knowledge in all their financial operations.

The steep progression of estate taxation is aimed especially at these new fortunes acquired through successful speculation. To President Hoover it was a moral task of government to expropriate "ill-gotten gains from the market speculator." To public opinion, it is the proper function of government to "retrieve" or at least share in the profits from speculation.

According to some able economists, the current inflation is bound to accelerate. They are convinced that material production will become increasingly difficult, that capital will be lost and consumed. Rapidly changing prices and costs will create uncertainty, confusion, or even chaos; and government will further aggravate matters with taxes and controls. It is not surprising, therefore, that the most flexible and capable entrepreneurs turn away from material production and embark upon speculation, which is the most important and rewarding economic activity in times of crisis. Speculators try to render the most urgent economic service needed at the time. They are quick to adjust their resources to the rapid changes in prices and markets suffering from chronic maladjustments due to the ever-changing monetary scene. Thus, they facilitate quicker and smoother readjustment and better allocation of economic resources to the most urgent needs of the public.

During rampant inflation it becomes economical to contract as many productive debts as possible. The speculator borrows other people's money, which is repaid later with depreciated currency. Instead of keeping large bank deposits, he finds it more advantageous to incur the highest possible debt with his bank. Of course, at all times he must maintain his liquidity to meet current obligations; he must always guard against the sudden calling of loans by his bank in moments of extreme credit stringency.

Inflation not only destroys income and wealth, but also redistributes them from millions of creditors to many debtors. Some businessmen, especially the young, aggressive entrepreneurs, understand this principle and utilize it to their advantage. They expand their enterprises or acquire new ones, merge with others or form new business structures — always building on debt. The inflation losses, suffered by banks and bond holders who finance the expansion, accrue as profits to these entrepreneurs who join the class of *nouveaux riches*. Occasionally the government reverses its monetary policy, deflates rather than inflates, or merely reduces the rate of monetary depreciation. Then these entrepreneurs may find themselves overextended. They may have to contract their operations, or liquidate some of their holdings. In fact, some may lose their fortunes even faster than they were made.

The survivors, who preserve their capital through booms and busts, deflation and inflation, confiscatory income and estate taxation, render invaluable services to society. They are preserving the productive capacity that will be needed to rebuild a productive economy when the upheaval ends. Surely, our age of inflation will come to an end. But when it finally does, our productive capacity will have been ravaged through overconsumption, wasteful costs, and bad investments. Only survivors with productive capital can hope to rebuild the great exchange system that is the American economy. Confiscatory estate levies would jeopardize the reconstruction.

The total impact of inflation and taxation on our daily lives is probably beyond anyone's comprehension. Government statistics readily confess to a share of 42 percent of total production as the real costs of government and some 10 percent to state and local governments. In addition, inflation annually transfers a large share of income and wealth from creditors to debtors. The economic, social and political effects of such massive transfer of economic well-being are incalculable. Yet, we may conclude, without much risk of contradiction, that the cost of government surpasses by far all other costs in our lives.

Chapter 3
HISTORY OF FEDERAL ESTATE TAXES

The states have a long and complicated experience with death duties. No matter how hard some may have tried to make this type of taxation yield substantial revenues, they generally failed because of the competition among various states. If one state imposed heavy death duties on large estates, others would endeavor to attract wealthy residents through friendlier tax climates. The hostile state would lose productive capital and thereby invite stagnation and poverty, while the more congenial states would prosper from the influx of productive capital. The competition of fifty sovereign states severely reduces the use of death duties and many other levies, restrictions and devices.

This limitation of the states' taxing power has given rise to the demand that the federal government should pre-empt the field. Although the federal government has tried in earnest since 1924, it, too, has failed to make death duties yield substantial revenues. Rarely has it derived more than two percent of its total revenue from this source. In fiscal 1983 the U.S. Budget is estimating an estate and gift tax revenue of $5.9 billion, or less than 1 percent of total receipts. (*The Budget for 1983*, p. 4-2). This disappointing flow of revenue is encompassed by the same forces of competition that frustrate the states. The federal government faces the competition of foreign governments that are offering friendlier tax climates. Switzerland, for instance, which has few natural resources for industrial wealth, has succeeded in building great national wealth on a capital market that offers reliable tax havens to the refugee capital of the world. The same considerations that cause some American millionaires to reside in Nevada, which levies no state death duties, have brought large family fortunes to Switzerland, seeking refuge in Swiss banks and numbered accounts.[9] Furthermore, the United States itself offers some avenues of escape for personal wealth, such as tax-exempt foundations

---

[9]William S. Sager, "Practicability of Uniform Death and Gift Tax Laws," in *National Tax Journal*, (Dec. 1957), pp. 361-369.

and trusts, which are discussed further below. But above all, it must not be overlooked that death duties bring forth their most pernicious effects long before they are levied. In most cases the duties reach merely a small fraction of the productive wealth that existed before death had to be contemplated. In preparation for the tax incidence, wealth, wherever possible, tends to change its form, move from more productive uses to less productive or even unproductive employment, such as government securities, or maybe consumed entirely. The very purpose of "estate planning" is to minimize the duty.

Such has been the experience of the federal government whenever it resorted to this type of exaction. In 1797, the federal government levied its first stamp tax on transmission of decedent estates, with a maximum rate of one-half of one percent. The Federalists had pledged the federal government to a heavy expenditure program, mainly on national defense. As these expenditures mounted, together with high interest obligations on the federal debt, the structure of federal finances threatened to topple. Therefore, several taxes were added to the revenue system, including a stamp tax on legal documents of property transfer. The law was repealed in 1802 when Thomas Jefferson's administration drastically cut expenditures and abolished all unpopular taxes. The stamp tax was too difficult to administer, was easy to evade, and yielded little in revenue.[10]

A new attempt at tapping this source of revenue was made during the Civil War. In 1862, Congressional and Treasury ingenuity was devising a comprehensive federal tax system. Every tax that could be conceived was levied; every citizen who could be reached was taxed. A catch-all revenue measure introduced inheritance taxation. At first, it applied only to transfers of personal property. While rates were proportional as to amount, they were graduated from three-quarters of one percent to five percent, according to the relationship of the recipient to the deceased. In 1864 the tax was broadened to include transfers of real property. In 1870, when the machinery of federal war finance was being gradually demobilized, inheritance taxes were ended along with other emergency levies.[11]

---

[10]Shultz and M. R. Caine, *Financial Development of the United States,* New York: Prentice-Hall, 1957, pp. 117 *et seq.*

[11]*Ibid.,* pp. 309 *et seq.*

A 2 percent inheritance tax was imposed as an element of the federal Income Tax Act of 1894. The courts held that law unconstitutional.

Again, during the Spanish-American War the U.S. Congress resorted to death taxation. It imposed a tax that was both an estate tax and an inheritance tax. Its rates were progressive relative to the size of the decedent's total estate, and to the relationship of the beneficiaries to the decedent. But the courts soon held the estate tax progression unconstitutional, which made the tax an ordinary inheritance tax, like its predecessors. It was repealed four years later, when the emergency had passed.

In 1916, when federal expenditures in preparation for the entrance of the United States into World War I were rising, a revenue act introduced the present federal estate tax. It differed from its predecessors in that it was never to be repealed, but raised frequently, although the emergency for which it was levied passed by 1918. In contrast to earlier death levies, it did not take the form of inheritance levies on the various heirs and beneficiaries, but was levied on the entire estate as left by the deceased. The act provided for an exemption of $50,000, and for progression on estates in excess of this amount. The rates ranged from 1 to 10 percent, with the maximum rate applying to estates in excess of $5,000,000.[12]

The estate tax of 1916 constitutes an important milestone in the history of federal death levies. What began as an emergency levy, imposed briefly and moderately, has evolved as a permanent instrument of economic and social policy. In the following years it was to be applied with ever greater severity. Its progression was sharpened to 40 percent in 1924, reduced to 20 percent in 1926, raised to 45 percent in 1932, and after further increases in 1934, 1935 and 1940, was boosted to 77 percent in 1941, a rate which remained in effect until 1976. The Tax Reform Act of 1976 reduced the maximum rate to 70 percent, but increased the gift tax rate substantially, unifying the estate and gift taxes so that a single progressive rate schedule was applied to cumulative gifts and bequests.

The Economic Recovery Tax Act of 1981 provided tempo-

---

[12]William J. Shultz and C. Lowell Harris, *American Public Finance*. New York: Prentice Hall, 1949, p. 486.

rary relief by reducing the maximum estate and gift tax rates from 70 percent on taxable estates over $5,000,000 to 50 percent on taxable estates over $2,500,000, in 5 percent increments over a four-year period. But this relief, at its best, granted merely a reprieve from the relentless pressures of inflation that is eroding the value of the tax credits and lifting estates and gifts into higher brackets. A 5 percent tax-rate reduction may be offset by a 10 percent inflation that increases the value of the taxable estate by 10 percent or more. In recent years of double-digit inflation the value rose more than 10 percent per year. And there is no indication whatever that inflation will abate in the coming years.

Intellectual Roots

Such policies of confiscatory taxation did not spring from despotic government or arbitrary administrations. In a democratic society they are the ripe fruits of ideas and ideologies that were devised by a few persuasive thinkers and writers swaying the majority of voters. The explanations and theories of a few thought-leaders tend to become the policies of freely-elected politicians who enact the laws and commit the instruments of government power to the realization of their second-hand ideas.

Throughout most of the 19th century the ideals of the private property order, commonly called capitalism, were accepted without question or hesitation. The teachings of American economists, such as Amasa Walker, Francia A. Walker, and William Graham Sumner, were popular and generally guided government policies. There was, however, no uniformity of thought. They frequently disagreed on the great economic problems of their time, notably on the tariff and on monetary matters. But they unhesitatingly agreed on the desirability of individual freedom and private property in economic production.

During the 1880's however, a new era in American economic thought became clearly visible. Henry George's *Progress and Poverty*, which had appeared in 1879, aroused great interest and stimulated ardent debates. As the most popular book on economics ever published up to that time, it exerted considerable influence on public attitudes.[13]

---

[13]Cf. *Progress and Poverty*. New York: Modern Library, 1916.

George's book and other writings denounced *laissez-faire* capitalism for fostering landed monopolies. As the country is settled and land passes into private ownership, Henry George reasoned, landowners become wealthy through the mere possession of land in growing communities, while wages and return on capital decline. As the increased value of the land is attributable to the activity of the community, it should be confiscated through taxation and thus returned to the community. His hostility towards profits on land naturally bred a general hostility towards all "unearned increments," and thus towards the very profit system itself.

The seeds of hostility which Henry George was sowing received strong nourishment from the "new economics" that came from abroad. It invaded the American colleges and universities and was an offshoot of the German Historical School. In 1885 the American Economic Association was founded to replace the abstract deductive economics of the English Classical School with historical investigation. It advocated a broadening of the functions of the state, labor regulation and legislation, and progressive taxation of "unearned" income and wealth. Under the leadership of university professors, such as R. T. Ely, S. N. Patten, H. B. Adams, and E. R. A. Seligman, it became the center of the "new thought." Its statement of principles, as prepared by Professor Ely, sounds "modern" even today, almost one hundred years later:

"1. We regard the State as an agency whose positive assistance is one of the indispensable conditions of human progress.

"2. We believe that political economy as a science is still in an early stage of its development. While we appreciate the work of former economists, we look not so much to speculation as to the historical and statistical study of actual conditions of economic life for the satisfactory accomplishment of that development.

"3. We hold that the conflict of labor and capital has brought into prominence a vast number of social problems, whose solution requires the united efforts, each in its own sphere, of the church, of the state, and of science.

"4. In the study of the industrial and commercial policy of governments we take no partisan attitude. We believe in a progressive development of economic conditions, which must be met by a corresponding development of legislative policy."[14]

In spite of their ambiguity, these principles indicate the transition in social and economic thought that was beginning to be felt in public opinion and government policy. The new "progressive" leaders exerted their powerful influence towards government regulation of monetary matters, of big business, and of the railways. They laid the intellectual groundwork for progressive taxation of income and wealth.

A few years later, they were supported by a new breed of social and political writers, the so-called "Institutionalists." Their mentor, Thorstein Veblen, levelled devastating charges at the market economy. Although he differed essentially with the analytical approach applied by Karl Marx, he concurred with Marx in most of his conclusions.

Veblen's most popular book, *The Theory of the Leisure Class*, first published in 1899, derided the capitalist economy as being riddled by conflict. Property rights, Veblen argued, enabled predatory groups to seize the production surplus and live in leisure. Plants and machines fall under the influence of moneyed interests who control production as absentee owners. They reap profits by restricting production and by price fixing. Through their greed and speculation, they throw the national economy into turmoil and depression. Their interests and practices clearly conflict with the common good.[15]

Although many differences may be found among the writers commonly classed as Institutional economists, they usually were in full agreement on basic principles. They believed that "social forces" and "group behavior," rather than individual choice and action, should be the object of economic analysis. They rejected theoretical deductions and economic laws on the grounds that human behavior is changing continuously and that economic knowledge is relative to time and place.

Institutional economics rose to its zenith during the 1920's

---

[14]As quoted by Lewis H. Haney in *History of Economic Thought*. New York: The Macmillan Co., 1949, p. 884.

[15]*The Theory of the Leisure Class*. New York: *The Modern Library*, 1934; also *The Theory of Business Enterprise*, first published in 1904; *Engineers and the Price System*, 1921; *Absentee Ownership and Business Enterprise in Recent Times*, 1923.

and 1930's. Writers such as J. R. Commons, W. C. Mitchell, J. M. Clark, and S. H. Slichter received great attention and acclaim. When Franklin D. Roosevelt became President in 1933, he took with him to Washington several advisors who embraced Institutional economics. They shaped the policies known as the "New Deal."

Many others openly advocated the immediate abolition of the private property order. There were the socialists, whose roots were deep in the teaching of Karl Marx and other revolutionaries of the 19th century. The soil for orthodox Marxism was never very fertile in America, because the working and living conditions of the American workers continually improved. Wages rose rapidly. In fact, they became the highest in the world in 1913. Consumer prices declined, and many a worker rose from rags to riches. This made it rather difficult for the Socialist Party of Eugene V. Debs to espouse the Marxian doctrines of class struggle, exploitation, and the workers' impoverishment. And yet, the Party grew steadily in membership and influence. Its presidential vote, with Debs as candidate, reached 900,000 in 1912. In the 1924 election its presidential candidate, Senator Robert M. LaFollette of Wisconsin, received nearly 5,000,000 votes.

Since 1928 Norman Thomas, writer, lecturer, former Presbyterian minister, served as the Party's new standard bearer. Although he repeatedly ran for the highest political office, his popular support never again attained the strength of 1924. The Roosevelt Administration embodied in its "New Deal" many immediate demands of the Socialist Party platform in the fields of social security, housing, public power, labor-management relations, and taxation. As a result of the ideological changes in the Democratic Party as well as the Republican opposition, many followers of socialism gave active support to the two major parties, which caused the Socialist Party to decline.

In eclectic fashion, many a prominent man in commerce and industry accepted some parts of the progressive program. Even the richest man on earth in his time, Andrew Carnegie, made a strong case against hereditary transmission of wealth. "Wealth left to young men, as a rule, is disadvantageous," he wrote in his widely-read *Gospel of*

Wealth.[16] "Lives of poverty and struggle are advantageous." Coming from the greatest industrialist of the time, who in the eyes of the progressives was a despised "robber barron," this plea for poverty had a strange sound. His stand against hereditary transmission of wealth rang like an open admission of "ill-gained" income and wealth.

William Howard Taft, the 27th president, took up the case for a graduated estate tax in his 1909 inaugural address. Pointing at England where the levies were heavy, he hoped that the United States would follow on the road to social fairness and justice. But he was doubtful of the constitutionality of his suggestions. Therefore Taft urged that the whole matter of taxation be settled once and for all by constitutional amendment. Five years later, in 1913, the Sixteenth Amendment became basic law in the United States. This opened the door to progressive income and estate taxation, and ushered in a new age: "The Congress shall have the power to levy and collect taxes on incomes, from whatever source derived, without apportionment among the several States, and without regard to any census or enumeration."

In the heated Presidential election of 1912, William Howard Taft was the "conservative" Republican candidate who was defeated by two "progressives" — Theodore Roosevelt, the leader of the Progressive Party, and Woodrow Wilson, the Democratic candidate. If a "conservative" was capable of spearheading such basic changes as the Sixteenth Amendment, the "progressives" in time would achieve much more.

Herbert Hoover, the 31st president, felt strongly about taxing and spending. His administration is remembered for having doubled the burden of federal taxation in 1932, at the very depth of the Great Depression, thus aggravating and prolonging the suffering. To him, the capital gains tax was a levy that took "ill-gotten gains from the market speculator." He personally urged his Secretary of the Treasury to prepare bills that would double the income and estate taxes. "I believe," President Hoover wrote in a memorandum, "that the estate tax, in moderation, is one of the most economically and socially desirable — or even necessary — of all taxes." In his *Memoirs* he later added: "The American people have from the earliest moments been alive to the evils of

---

[16]Cambridge, Mass: The Belknap Press, 1962, p. 56 (First published in 1900).

inherited economic power. Several million dollars is economic power and too often it falls into the hands of persons of little intention to use that power for public benefit either in expansion of enterprise and employment or for public services. It is the breeding ground of playboys and playgirls of morally obnoxious and degenerating character."[17]

With such beliefs and convictions, why did the President urge a mere doubling of the levy? Total confiscation would have been in order.

Other American presidents from Franklin Delano Roosevelt to Jimmy Carter fully concurred with President Hoover and, therefore, exerted their great influence toward ever higher estate taxation.[18] Their successful efforts were fortified by yet another popular policy they eagerly pursued: the expansion and depreciation of currency, which is inflation. Since the days of Herbert Hoover goods prices have risen nearly tenfold, which caused the value of more and more estates in terms of depreciating dollars to soar to taxable levels. The estate tax which was meant to lay waste to "the breeding ground of playboys and playgirls" gradually advanced to the frontyards of farmers, ranchers and small businessmen. If it is true that double-digit inflation in time must give way to triple-digit inflation, the death duties will soon overwhelm the estates of most Americans.

---

[17]*The Memoirs of Herbert Hoover*, "The Great Depression." New York: Macmillan & Co., 1952, p. 136.

[18]Prevailing contemporary thought is no less hostile toward personal wealth than it was during the 1920's and 1930's. For a brief description and analysis see Chapter VII.

Chapter 4
DEATH TAXES AS
WEALTH EQUALIZERS

Taxation is one of the most potent instruments of political and economic reform. It is a political tool that can change the political and economic system, redistribute the fruits of all our labors, and inflict oppression on some or all people. In the often quoted words of Justice Marshall, "The power to tax is the power to destroy." And, in the words of Edmund Burke: "Taxing is an easy business. Any projector can contrive new impositions; any bungler can add to the old; but is it altogether wise to have no other bounds to your imaginations than the patience of those who are to bear them?"

Government endeavors to improve the position of the poor and indigent. But the tax programs that are to provide the revenue for transfer payments and social services actually are aggravating the plight of the poor. After all, taxes like the corporate income tax, the estate tax, and many other business taxes imposed on the rich are taxes on economic production. They consume the very capital which creates jobs through investments, improves production and working conditions, and thereby raises wage rates. To advocate higher taxes on the rich, most of whom are highly productive businessmen and investors, is to expropriate the very means of capital investment that afford jobs and better living conditions for the poor. It is in the vital interest of the poor that there be wealthy promoters and investors who do not consume all their income. If allowed to, this group may build factories and stores, shops and other business establishments, all of which provide jobs and income. This is why, contrary to popular belief, *progressive death duties do not diminish economic inequality; they are powerful instruments for creating it.*

In a market system with private property in the means of production, a rich man's wealth mainly consists of means of production that employ labor and produce economic goods. A small fraction of his wealth may be spent on consumers' goods for his own comfort and enjoyment. The worker, whose income is spent on consumers' goods only and whose worldly possessions may consist of such goods only, may have a standard of living resembling the capitalist. Admittedly, his house, car, clothing, etc. may be of lesser quality than those of the latter, but they are similar in service and amenity. The similarity of both standards of living gives rise to a classless society.[19]

What happens to this similarity when productive capital is lost, dissipated, or consumed by spendthrift government? With every dollar of net consumption, the worker's productivity must decline, as must his wages and living conditions. But the rich man's consumptive wealth may not be affected at all. Thus, the similarity between worker and capitalist gives way to growing inequality and emerging social classes.

A specific example may illustrate the point. A tenfold millionaire who is busily managing his enterprise is using one hundred thousand dollars for his own comfort and enjoyment, for his house, cars, furniture, clothing, etc. His consumptive wealth is only one percent of his total wealth. If, for the sake of economic equality, most of his total wealth should be seized and consumed, the laborer's productivity and living conditions will fall immediately, while the rich man's consumptive wealth may not be touched at all. The inequality will increase with every dollar of capital consumption. It is even conceivable that a society bent on self-destruction may seize and consume more and more productive capital until the worker faces hunger and misery from lack of production. The rich man, however, may manage through talent, industry, or thrift to preserve the tiny share of wealth that affords him comfortable living conditions. The ultimate inequality emerges when laborers perish from hunger and want, while rich men cling to their remaining possessions.

The poor countries in Asia, Africa, and Latin America offer living proof of the chasm of social classes. They lack the facilities of production that make human labor more productive. With primitive tools and equipment, man and beast

---

[19]Cf. Ludwig von Mises, *Human Action*. Chicago: Henry Regnery Co., 1966, p. 840 *et seq.*

struggle with nature for the bare means of subsistence. They labor from dawn to dusk in constant fear of droughts and famines. Millions are living in the abject poverty which has been man's steady companion since the beginning of time.[20] But in their midst a few individuals always manage to live in comfort, even in luxury, as military and political leaders. Their position affords economic and social power; their wealth is derived from the state. It consists of landed estates and city mansions, and all the luxuries the world can offer. If the position should yield a surplus of income over conspicuous consumption, more personal wealth is accumulated in Swiss Bank vaults in the form of precious metals, jewelry, art objects, or other valuable items. Rarely, if ever, is it invested in means of production.

When we compare the inequality of social classes in such countries with the economic inequality in highly productive countries in which productive capital is privately owned and created, we are tempted to deduce a basic economic law or principle. It may be formulated as follows: *Economic and social inequality is inversely related to economic productivity, income and wealth.* Inequality tends to grow with declining labor productivity; it tends to diminish with rising labor productivity.

When applied to confiscatory estate taxation, or any other government policy that causes capital consumption, this principle permits us to conclude: Any policy measure that takes capital from the rich to facilitate consumption actually aggravates economic and social inequality and creates a society of economic and social classes.[21] Progressive estate taxation, in particular, aggravates the inequality. Therefore, anyone genuinely concerned about economic inequality must favor a summary abolition of the tax.

In final analysis, the crucial question of who holds an anterior title to property — its creator or the state, must be raised and answered. When the state is the source of prop-

---

[20]Cf. E. Parmalee Prentice, *Hunger and History.* New York: Harper & Bros., 1939.

[21]Cf. Gottfried Dietze, *In Defense of Property.* Chicago: Henry Regnery Co., 1963, p. 128 *et seq.* Also Leonard E. Read, *The Love of Liberty,* The Foundation for Economic Education, Inc., 1975, p. 28 *et seq.*; also his *Anything That's Peaceful,* FEE, 1964, p. 32 *et seq.* Edmund A. Opitz, *Religion and Capitalism: Allies, Not Enemies.* New Rochelle, N.Y.: Arlington House, 1970, p. 231 *et seq.*

erty through conquest or expropriation of previous owners, the state holds the first title upon any estate; those who come afterwards have a subordinate, derivative title. However, where individual effort and thrift are the source of property the title belongs to its creator, in life and death.

Chapter 5
EFFECTS ON PREDECESSORS

A voluminous literature deals with the incidence of death levies. Always pressed for more revenue to cover ever rising expenditures, the taxing authorities are continually devising new pleas and arguments for ever higher rates. They find eager support from sociologists and economists who would like to reform the economic system by abolishing, or at least reducing, the existing inequalities in income and wealth. Blinded by their specific objectives, they rarely raise the questions of who actually bears the burden of death taxes and what their economic and social consequences ultimately will be. But when such questions are raised, their answers usually confirm their basic objectives.

Their favorite doctrine of incidence of death duties is attributed to the English philosopher-economist Jeremy Bentham. According to Bentham, death taxes are completely painless as they impose no burden upon anyone. By the time the tax is imposed the deceased creator of the estate lies in his grave, unaffected by the levy, while his successors suffer no loss of wealth they never owned. They may have a legal expectation, but no economic claim. If they expect to own the estate, and then are called upon to give up a part, they actually feel the pain of the tax. But if the estate should be *partitioned*, no sensation of loss is felt. According to Bentham, "the more is taken under the name of tax, the more burthensome the measure, as everybody knows; at the same time, the more is taken for the public under the name of *partition*, so long as an equal or not much more than equal share is left to the individual, the farther the measure from being burthensome, because the farther from being considered as a tax . . . Instead of the tax, a law of inheritance, giving the public fifty percent upon certain successions, the burthen may be next to nothing; pass a law of inheritance giving the public the whole, the burthen vanishes altogether."[22]

Seldom has a man's thought been so directly and widely translated into public policy as that of Jeremy Bentham. His disciples credited him with nearly all the important British

---

[22]*The Works of Jeremy Bentham*, Edinburgh, 1843, Vol. II, p. 590.

reforms of the first half of the nineteenth century. Guided by his utilitarian ideal of the greatest happiness for the greatest number, he spearheaded an admirable reform of civil and criminal law and paved the way for needed parliamentary reform. But his social ideal of subsistence, abundance, security, and equality led him to put government in the center of his economic system. He visualized a welfare state with free education, guaranteed employment, minimum wages, sickness benefits, and old-age insurance. His proposal of painless "partition" meant to facilitate the redistribution program.

Bentham's doctrine of death-duty incidence is probably one of the most shallow dabblings of economic thought in economic literature. Playing with words he wants his readers to believe that a confiscatory exaction called "tax" is painful, but that it is painless when called "partition." His reasoning is like that of a surgeon who informs his patient that the loss of his limb would be tragic, but that its amputation would be of no importance.

The English economist Arthur C. Pigou placed the incidence of death levies solely on the accumulator of wealth. Death levies, according to Pigou, merely are "back" property taxes borne by the deceased alone. While he pays property taxes throughout life, he must allow for a lump sum payment as back payment or arrearage when he leaves this life. Death duties "are occasional property taxes, thus standing in contrast with annual property taxes. Instead of collecting a relatively small sum from each property every year, they collect a large sum from each property at intervals averaging about thirty years and associated with the death of the proprietor."[23]

Pigou looked at death taxes from the point of view of the tax collector: property yields an annual revenue amounting to a small percentage of the property value — and once in a lifetime he can gather a larger percentage. But such a perspective does not answer the question of incidence, on whom the tax burden must ultimately fall. A tax is a burdensome charge, an obligation which only a living person can meet. Even legal entities, such as corporations, foundations, and trusts only pay taxes for their owners or beneficiaries, who are the ultimate victims of the levy.

---

[23] A. C. Pigou, *A Study in Public Finance*, London: Macmillan & Co., 1929.

This fact seems to support the common view that the incidence of death taxes falls on the successors only, as they are deprived of some economic benefits they otherwise would have received. We share this view in all those cases where the predecessor unexpectedly departed from this life, without any preparations or provisions for the disposition of his estate. While youth may frequently be guilty of such shortsightedness, it rarely leaves estates that are of interest to tax collectors. The creators of taxable estates mostly give thought and effort to the impact of the levy that may greatly impair their life's work.

The view presented by this writer is that the burden of death levies falls on three parties — the predecessor, the successor, and the public. The predecessor may be affected by his anticipation of the levy and may make adjustments in his actions while he is still alive. The heir and beneficiary is affected in a negative way, as he comes into possession of a greatly reduced estate that differs in substance and productivity from the original estate. Regardless of the effects on the heirs, we are convinced that most predecessors are mindful of a tax designed to bestow a large share of their life's achievements on the government.

The Work-Leisure Choice

The vast majority of individuals would like to improve their economic conditions. This is why many save and invest in order to enjoy greater income and material well-being in the future. They basically follow Benjamin Franklin's advice that "if you know how to spend less than you get you have the philosopher's stone," and are mindful of his warning that "a man may, if he knows not how to save as he gets, keep his nose all his life to the grindstone and die not worth a groat after all." They do care about building an estate.

A death tax may affect a person's choice between work and leisure. He may stay on his job in order to add more to his estate, or he may choose to retire. If he is strongly motivated to leave his family secure in income and wealth, he may continue to work as long and hard as he can, in order to increase his estate. The thought of a death levy that may spoil his hope and ambition may keep him on the job until the last day of his life. However, if the levy becomes too onerous to overcome through harder work or great thrift, if the futility of his efforts becomes apparent, he may prefer retirement over further work and accumulation. Or he may direct his efforts toward tax avoidance or evasion in order to leave more wealth to his family.

The size of the estate may greatly affect the work-leisure choice. Relatively small estates that are subject to low rates of death duties can be safeguarded through additional efforts by the accumulator of wealth. Larger estates that were built by several generations of highly productive merchants and industrialists, cannot easily be protected through personal productivity and thrift. Other avenues must be found.

The thought of an onerous death levy may cause a person to seek vacation or retirement. After all, the price of leisure is reduced by a tax that seriously hampers his productive efforts. The price of a world trip or Florida retirement is reduced by 50 percent if the estate tax collector is waiting to claim 50 percent. As leisure and consumption become less expensive, many individuals may choose to have more.

But even if we should discount the possibility of estate taxes seriously affecting the working habits of people, we still must face the fact that many may redirect their efforts. The captain of industry may choose to become a dollar-a-year man in the State Department, a philanthropist for mental health, a trustee of the community hospital, or member of the school board. Or he may finally find the time to realize his childhood ambition of rebuilding and driving a Rolls-Royce. That is, the industrialist with exceptional productivity ceases to add to his estate, but instead enters occupations in which he produces very little.

It is difficult to estimate the magnitude of this shift to leisure and play in recent decades. Many millions of elderly people are living "in retirement," waiting for Social Security benefits and pensions, consuming their savings, and idling their days away searching for fun and play. Never in the history of man has the older generation contributed so little to human improvement and demanded so much from the younger generations as today. They are everywhere, congregating in retirement homes provided by state and federal government, in special settlements and communities, in their favorite cities and sunshine states. They are giving our age its ominous characteristics: massive redistribution of income and wealth from one social class to another, and the consumption of productive wealth by the classes of leisure and political favor.

This is not to imply that confiscatory estate taxation is the sole cause of this development. It is, first of all, a symptom of a new morality that places present comfort and pleasure in the center of man's concern. Contemporary man seeks gratification *now*, with gusto and *joie de vivre*. Confiscatory death duties merely reinforce his conviction that there is no tomorrow and that "you cannot take it with you." The older generation of Americans, imbued with the ideal of leisure and pleasure and the ideology of economic benefits by political force, is setting a portentious example to the coming generations.

Consumption Choice

Few young people consciously allow death-tax considerations to determine their consumption patterns. For middle-aged and older people, the same considerations that enter into the work-leisure choice may affect the saving-consumption choice.

For highly productive individuals whose estates will be sizeable, the temptation to change their consumption pattern is nearly irresistable. Why should they continue to labor and invest their savings in productive enterprises that will be decimated and liquidated for estate-tax purposes as soon as death forces a change of management? The successful entrepreneur may decide to engage in eleemosynary spending that amounts to pure consumption. The million-dollar gift to a racial minority group merely reduces the net estate after death taxes by the percentage not claimed by the tax collector. Or he may cover the deficits of his alma mater, which may grant him an honorary doctor's degree. His generous gift that sustains or supplements the professors' patterns of consumption may reduce the net value of his estate by relatively little. Obviously, death-tax considerations cause him to be consumption-oriented, and may make him aspire for prestige and public acclaim that usually are bestowed on generosity.

Estate-tax considerations not only affect the size of an estate but also its composition. They greatly influence present owners in selecting a type of holdings that can be marketed and distributed easily. If the estate consists of marketable securities, such as U.S. Treasury obligations or General Motors common stock, the difficulties of liquidation are minor. But a highly specialized family enterprise cannot easily be liquidated to pay the death levies. Therefore, while still in his prime, the man who is both successful and mindful of his children prepares financially for his demise by selling out. He must avoid leaving his business to his widow or heirs and the tax collector. His widow usually knows little of its management and operation. And she could hardly hope to sell it profitably within the period of time allowed for tax payment. Therefore, the businessman endeavors to sell his enterprise under conditions as favorable as possible and then reinvest the proceeds in Treasury obligations. The death duty thus eliminates an independent enterprise and channels productive capital into government debt. Thousands of small and medium-sized family businesses thus disappear every year, while the giant corporations continue to grow.

In anticipation of confiscatory death levies the present estate owner may also take more risk in his investment decisions than he normally would. Having accumulated his wealth in tedious management of a family enterprise, the elderly estate owner may finance risky ventures, such as new inventions or the drilling of oil wells in unproven fields. If successful, the net estate will grow a little; if unsuccessful, it will shrink by the investment minus the estate tax. Obviously, an onerous death levy induces investors to take more total risk, which often entails business losses and capital consumption.

Many estate owners are tempted to convert their productive assets that yield incomes into consumptive assets for their own enjoyment. They may acquire several luxury residences with swimming pools and helicopters, skiing lodges and hunting ranches, or sail the oceans on luxury yachts. Or they may finally indulge in the enjoyment of aesthetic goods, such as expensive paintings, rare books, and other valuable collections of art objects. Such expenditures may not reduce the value of an estate through pure consumption, but they rarely cause it to grow.

It is difficult to surmise the massive consumption of wealth that is precipitated by death duties. Surely, it is commonplace in the private property order that the luxuries of one generation become the necessities of the next. The private bath was one of the greatest luxuries in Medieval times; it was largely confined to the wealthy during the 19th century; today it is one of the necessities of civilized life. Nevertheless, the enormous growth of luxury industries in recent years is more than just an inevitable concomitant of the growth of wealth in a capitalistic economy. Today, productivity rates are actually declining, the levels of living of working people are falling, and yet, there is more conspicuous consumption than ever before.

The wealth-consumption effort on the part of elderly entrepreneurs and capitalists is visible everywhere in the United States. New million-dollar yachts are manufactured every day, in boom and recession; magnificent furs and jewelry are bought at dazzling prices; executive jets are crowding the skies without apparent regard for operating expenses and capital costs. And yet, most of this conspicuous spending becomes quite "economical" if tax considerations enter the cost calculation. Income taxes together with estate taxation may reduce the net costs to owners to bargain rates.

But there is more to the luxury craze than beautiful yachts and executive jets. The unbridled real estate boom in resort and retirement centers has its psychological roots in a nationwide retirement and wealth-consuming mania. Countless productive businesses are liquidated all over the country so that aging widows may enjoy the view over Waikiki beach from their million-dollar bungalows. The fantastic housing boom in Florida, California and Hawaii in recent years was not just the effect of wasteful spending by a few eccentric millionaires, nor the inevitable consequence of governmental restrictions that favor old residents at the expense of newcomers, but was built, and continues to build on a nationwide mentality of early retirement and estate consumption. Confiscatory estate taxation levied over half a century has succeeded in imparting a new mentality that prefers pride and luxury to labor and thrift.

Chapter 6
EFFECTS ON SUCCESSORS

By the time the wealth of a predecessor comes into the hands of his heirs, all crucial decisions have been made. The tax collector has taken his share, the executors have claimed theirs, and the heirs receive what is left. Their total asset position has been reduced by prior claims. It is true, the successor now owns more wealth than he did before. But his economic position and living conditions need not have improved by the inheritance. The widow who now holds the legal title to property may be greatly reduced in circumstances by the loss of her husband. The child now in possession of deeds and titles may be helpless without the father. In all such cases the estate tax greatly aggravates the disaster that has befallen them. In fact, this is true in nearly all cases of wealth transfer. The founder of family wealth is a person of exceptional productivity. The fortune he creates consists of means of production that yield income, give employment, and serve consumers. No member of his family is enriched by his demise, no matter how much they should inherit from him. The Ford family did not benefit when the great founder passed from the scene, nor did the Rockefellers when John D. departed this life, nor the thousands of workers who found employment in the family enterprises or the millions of consumers served by them.

What the government takes, the successors do not obtain. The family spending power is reduced because its net worth is reduced. The tax levies may cut into both consumption and investment, depending on the size of inheritance and on personal factors. As family wealth mainly consists of capital assets that are employed in production, an estate tax primarily falls on such assets. The tax causes their liquidation while it rarely touches family consumptive wealth, which the heirs may want to preserve as long as possible. Having grown accustomed to a certain life style, they may continue their consumption expenditures as before, although the productive base has been reduced severely. They may even consume capital substance and thus compound the economic effects of the death levy.

Some heirs may want to repair the damage inflicted on the family fortune by creating new capital through personal productivity and thrift. They may reduce their consumption expenditures in order to replenish the capital lost to government. But no matter what their reaction to the inheritance, the death levies decimate the productive capital of an enterprise. For a society that is striving to alleviate poverty, create employment, and raise the levels of living, the death duties are utterly counter-productive. To tax and consume what generations have built and accumulated is to reduce labor productivity and individual income.

Death taxes do not immediately and visibly destroy such capital equipment as steel mills, railroads, or refineries, but they force the heirs or owners to sell all or part of the taxed estate in order to raise the cash needed for the tax payment. This cash is liquid capital consumed by government visibly and noisily in the form of salary and welfare checks, subsidies, benefits, federal housing and buildings. The loss in productive investments — the factories and stores not built, the oil wells not drilled — will never be seen. Everyone loses when government consumes productive capital. Consumers must pay higher prices for fewer goods. Workers earn less for their efforts. All lose but the beneficiaries of the transfer process.

We must not overlook that this capital consumption is compounded by an army of tax accountants and attorneys who are thriving on the administration and distribution of estates. These indirect costs of taxation often decimate productive capital as effectively as the death duties themselves. Well-paid advisers send money abroad in search of reliable tax havens. Billions of dollars are spent each year for devising and administering trusts and foundations. The legal profession is multiplying, and the foundations become bureaucratic, heavy with tax attorneys and accountants who wage defensive battles with their counterparts in government, all frittering away productive capital. And the capital that escapes this consumption may be mismanaged by expensive committees of investment experts.

Death duties that decimate family wealth diminish the heir's entrepreneurial inclination and capacity. He may be more cautious in money management than his wealthy predecessor and unwilling to take risks in investing. The same may be true of the board of trustees that is managing the foundation wealth. Consequently, business may lose risk capital that is needed for new ventures, new technology or unproven processes of production, or mere readjustments of production to new situations. The economy thus loses the great flexibility and dynamic strength which characterize the unhampered private enterprise order.

When confiscatory estate taxes greatly reduce the economic circumstances of heirs, they must reduce their contributions to charitable and philanthropic endeavors. In anticipation of death levies, the predecessors may increase their contributions lest the government receive the lion's share. The successors, however, have no choice but to curtail their giving. On balance, the sum of charitable works by modest holdings of wealth tends to be smaller than that of greater accumulations. Consequently, schools and hospitals, and countless eleemosynary endeavors depend to an ever greater degree on government programs and support. The diversity of charitable, cultural and philanthropic pursuits supported by private donations thus gives way to the uniformity of government undertakings, affected invariably by political and ideological considerations. In the end, government may attain monopoly position and power. But charity that proclaims its good deeds in political oratory and disburses funds seized from widows and heirs ceases to be charity.

A Widow's Tax

No study has ever been made on the sexual distribution of the decedents who must bear the burden of death duties. But it should be obvious that the burden falls mostly on widows. Female life expectancy at birth is presently calculated at 75.2 years; that of the male is given at 67.4 years. (Division of Vital Statistics, National Center for Health Statistics, 1972 Data.) Furthermore, as it is the custom for wives to be younger than their husbands, wives must expect to survive their husbands by more than 8 years. Therefore, we must conclude, without much risk of contradiction, that estate tax obligations fall preponderantly on widows, the surviving partners of wealth-creating units.

If the women's liberation movement ever had a just cause for complaint, the estate tax properly ranks high on the list of grievances. As the surviving partner, she must raise the money through liquidation of assets to pay the levies on her husband's estate. Frequently a friend or attorney of the decedent may act as the executor and liquidate the assets in her possession. If husband and wife hold property in joint tenancy, which is the natural arrangement in a life partnership, the entire value of their property is assumed to belong to the husband and is subject to estate taxes — unless she can prove that she inherited part of the estate, or held outside employment that permitted her to meet payments, or otherwise made legally recognizable contributions to the estate. Unless she can bring proof by cancelled checks, notes, paychecks of Social Security tax withholdings, she is assumed to have contributed nothing to the estate.[24]

The authors of tax laws do not realize that wives greatly contribute to the creation of family wealth. Along with their husbands they are increasing family net worth over the years. In all occupations and professions — on the farm, in all kinds of businesses — they contribute to the family success as thrifty partners, planners, executives, receptionists, bookkeepers, secretaries, etc. Yet, upon her husband's death she has to engage a lawyer to prove her contribution, and upon her death, the same property will be taxed again to the heirs — usually the children.[25]

Small Business

Everyone loses when government consumes productive capital. Yet, for the sake of economic equality, confiscatory death duties continue to destroy family wealth. When the duties fall on a large enterprise scarcely a word is said about the economic impact on the heirs, on employees and customers. If the popular news media should actually cover the

---

[24]In 1948 the marital deduction was introduced. It permitted a decedent to give up to one-half of his estate to a surviving spouse free of estate tax. The Tax Reform Act of 1976 modified the deduction by limiting it to 50 percent of the adjusted gross estate or $250,000, whichever was greater. The Economic Recovery Tax Act of 1981 provided an *unlimited* marital deduction of all interspousal transfers, during lifetime or at death. The act also provided that the estate of the first spouse to die will include one-half of the value of jointly-owned property, regardless of which spouse furnished the consideration for the acquisition of the property. Cf. Silverstein and Mullens, *Tax Management*, Washington, D.C., 1981, Part I, p. A-224.
[25]Laura Lane, "Let's Get Rid of the Widow's Tax" in the *Farm Journal*, Sept., 1975.

story, they may gloat about the "passing of an era." When the same fate befalls numerous small businessmen the estate tax is felt to be burdensome, although the tax rate may only amount to 30 percent. Actually, whether the tax levy falls on a small business or a large enterprise, the economic impact is basically the same although it may differ in degree. In both cases, all or part of the productive assets may need to be sold in order to pay the levy. As the rates on large estates are significantly higher, a larger percentage of the productive assets usually is sold, and more capital is transferred to government. The large business that was built by several generations of able entrepreneurs is more likely sold under the impact of a 50 percent capital levy.

This continuation of family wealth over several generations is especially objectionable to the equalizers.[26] The prosperous enterprise that is in the possession of one family throughout decades is their favorite target. Actually, neither the founder nor the successor enjoys any special privilege that allocates family wealth. In a competitive enterprise order, the heir to a business must continually manage its assets in the best service of customers. If he does so ably and successfully, he will preserve the business or even facilitate its growth. If he should neglect its management or supervision, or commit costly blunders, competition would soon inflict serious losses. As profits allocate capital to able entrepreneurs, so do losses take capital from incompetent heirs. They destroy a family enterprise in a few years and thereby make room for more able newcomers. From rags to riches, and back to rags in two or three generations — that seems to be the natural order of family ability and fortune. If, occasionally, family wealth is preserved beyond this limit, only extraordinary family talent over several generations accounts for such an achievment.

In an unhampered market order, competition quickly deprives an incompetent heir of his inherited fortune. But in a rigid command system that abhors and prevents competition and the rapid changes it causes, heirs may seek shelter for their fortunes in fully guaranteed government securities and tax-exempt obligations. They may withdraw from the exacting demands of competition by entrusting their funds

[26]Cf. Joseph A. Pechman, *Federal Tax Policy*. New York: W. W. Norton & Co., 1971, p. 206.

to the U.S. Treasury, which guarantees perpetuation of family wealth without effort. Even such government umbrellas are leaking badly today, as inflation is eroding the substance of the protected wealth. As inflation accelerates, family fortunes thus protected are gradually annihilated, and the rule of "rags to riches and back to rags in three generations" prevails once again.

Farm Property

Small farms and businesses have played an important role in American economic history. They have opened the continent, tamed the West, and supplied a rapidly increasing population with more products and services. They have given millions of Americans the opportunity to build meaningful lives by their own initiative and effort. With more than 5 million businesses and some 3 million farms, most of which are relatively small, Americans are enjoying higher wage rates and levels of living that are the envy of the world.

The impact of death duties probably is more severe on farming than on any other occupation. When the tax progression almost reached its present rates in 1935 (ranging from 2 percent to 70 percent), land values were greatly depressed and the average farm value with land and buildings probably did not exceed $5,000. Very few farmers were affected by the estate tax. The American Farm Bureau Federation estimates that in 1942 the average farm was selling for $6,100.[27] Since then the acreage of the average farm has grown substantially due to the application of more productive equipment. As output and productivity have risen, and agriculture recovered from the Great Depression, the price of farms has risen accordingly. It rose further due to inflation and the erosion of the purchasing power of the dollar. The amount of machinery and equipment required to operate a farm unit has soared to astonishing levels. As a result, estate taxation has become a serious threat to a great many farmers.

The market value of most farms probably exceeds half a million dollars today. It is no coincidence that the agricultural states now harbor the greatest concentration of mil-

---

[27]Statement of the American Farm Bureau Federation to the House Ways and Means Committee, presented by Allan Grant, President, on March 15, 1976.

lionaires. Inflation has made many farmers with 500 or more acres unexpected millionaires. According to a United States Trust Company report based on tax information from the Internal Revenue Service, the density of million-dollar wealth is greatest by far in Idaho, with 27 millionaires among each thousand residents. Other states seem to follow in the order of agricultural importance: North Dakota 8.88, Maine 6.94, Nebraska 6.75, Minnesota 5.72, Indiana 4.63, Iowa 4.59, Wisconsin 4.49, New Jersey 3.91, Connecticut and Montana 3.81. New York merely ranks 13th in this list, with 3 millionaires per thousand.[28]

The annual growth rate of millionaires seems to vary with the rate of inflation and increases in land prices. During double-digit rates the number is growing at an annual rate of about 15 percent. During years of single-digit inflation the number is growing at 10 percent or less. The growth due to inflation more than offsets the decline on account of death, distribution of assets among heirs, estate taxation, dissipation in anticipation of death, or just ordinary loss. Inflation continuously replenishes the class of Americans at whom estate taxation is specifically directed, by adding ever more farmers to the tax rolls.

Death duties impose heavy burdens especially on efficient commercial farming operations that do not have large amounts of liquid capital available to pay estate taxes. Many farmers are unaware of their potential estate tax liabilities, which catch many families by surprise after an unexpected death. Therefore, they fail to take advantage of the many provisions of tax avoidance used by others. Faced with high estate taxes, many heirs are forced to sell the family farm or ranch. If they should sell off some acreage in order to pay the levy, they frequently find themselves with too small an operating unit, whose production costs are much higher than those of competing farms of optimal size. Consequently they may face financial difficulties or even bankruptcy a few years later.

Many family farms are sold to corporations that are engaging in several different enterprises and are operating farm units. Every year thousands of farm heirs are vacating the land and seeking refuge in towns and cities, and large

---

[28]*New York Times*, Sept. 7, 1980.

corporations take their place in the country. But no matter how "professional" corporate management may be, it cannot replace the efficiency and frugality of the farming family. Farm output and yield decline, and losses may be suffered, which are offset by profits in other corporate operations. For the corporation, the operating loss may be a necessary expense for the opportunity to hold land as an excellent hedge against inflation and monetary destruction. But for the public as consumers of agricultural products, corporate inefficiency on the farm means fewer products and higher food prices.

Chapter 7
AVOIDANCE AND EVASION

The great majority of Americans do not yet have a federal estate tax problem. Their estates are below the level of the credit set by law. The Tax Reform Act of 1976, which unified the estate and gift taxes so that a single progressive rate schedule was applicable to cumulative gifts and bequests, had set a credit of $47,000, which made cumulative transfers of up to $175,625 tax exempt. The Economic Recovery Tax Act of 1981 raised the credit in stages to $62,800 in 1982, exempting $225,000; to $79,300 in 1983, exempting $275,000; to $96,300 in 1984, exempting $325,000; to $121,800 in 1985, exempting $400,000; to $155,800 in 1986, exempting $500,000; and to $192,800 in 1987 and thereafter, exempting $600,000. If inflation should rage on in the coming years as it did in previous years, these credits may depreciate faster in real terms than they are raised in nominal amounts, so that more estates will be taxed at higher and higher rates. By 1987, the neighborhood grocery store may exceed the exemption equivalent and be taxable as an estate. As federal and state death duties become more onerous, strenuous efforts are made by estate owners and their tax advisors to take advantage of all available routes of escape.

A simple device that permits untaxed transfer of considerable wealth to the next generation is giving wealth away prior to death. But such giving is generally taxable at estate and gift-tax rates except for a small "exclusion." From 1943 to 1981 the law allowed an annual gift tax exclusion of $3,000 per donee. The Economic Recovery Tax Act of 1981 raised this amount to $10,000. It also provided for an unlimited exclusion for amounts paid for medical expenses and school tuition, which may be used in addition to the $10,000 annual gift tax exclusion.

The use of this annual exclusion is an important estate planning tool, especially for younger donors with many children. Father and mother together may transfer $20,000 annually to each child and continue to bear their medical and educational expenses regardless of age. Over thirty years of faithful giving each child may receive $600,000 which, when productively invested and properly managed, may grow into a tidy sum. To be meaningful, this method of tax-free sharing of wealth with the coming generation must be practiced regularly, from the day the baby is born to the day the last parent departs this life. Obviously it offers no last-minute escape from onerous death levies.

This tax-free transfer of family wealth may be a simple matter where gifts are made from current income and invested in the name and for the benefit of children. The physician who otherwise would make hefty contributions to his own retirement fund, which would be taxable in his estate, makes $10,000 investments for each of his children. But such gifts create transfer problems where the income is meager and barely sufficient for current living expenses. The rancher, farmer or businessman may be worth a couple of million dollars, but may lack the income for any transfer. He must limit his giving to the productive assets that comprise his wealth. For that purpose he may form a partnership with his children and then transfer annually a percentage of his assets that amount to $10,000. Our rancher, farmer or businessman may give one percent to each of his children, provided his spouse consents to gift-splitting. In twenty years of faithful giving to five children the two-million dollar wealth is transferred completely to the young generation. Inflation that raises the value of the assets would delay this result.

Industrial, commercial, and agricultural wealth that is incorporated and represented by stock certificates of ownership can be transferred easily under the exclusion rule. The stock owner merely makes annual gifts of a number of shares, or fractions of shares, that are valued at $10,000. If a particular corporate form, such as a professional corporation, is unsuited for such stock transfer, a more suitable holding company may be built on top of the corporation. The owner of the holding company, which controls the voting power of other individual corporations, may make the desired stock gifts.

Many estate planners urge their clients to reduce estate tax liability through generous charitable giving. There is no limitation on the amount of the estate tax deduction; the full amount of any property passing to a qualified charity is tax-free, that is, gifts and bequests to religious, charitable, scientific, literary, or educational organizations. The tax savings derived from the use of deductions may actually mean genuine savings for the family.

Charitable giving is always suspect if it is deferred until death. He who waits until then is generous with another man's substance rather than his own. And yet, it may be advisable if the deductions mean greater security for the family or the alternative is confiscatory taxation. If government seizes the family wealth it undoubtedly will be used to replenish the public trough, which is corruptive and destructive. If a charitable organization receives the wealth it, too, is likely to consume its substance, but, by doing so, may afford gratuitous relief of any kind of distress. It may be brotherly love in action.

Many charitable organizations offering refuge from confiscatory estate taxation seem to rejoice about high tax rates that make charitable giving so attractive. To lower the rates or raise the exclusion, they contend, is to reduce the motivation for private giving. But such tendencies constitute merely shortrun manifestations of the flight of private capital from confiscation and consumption by government. Upon completion of this flight the rush must come to an end, leaving behind a depleted stock of private capital and an exhausted economy which, in the end, may destroy all incentives to private giving. Moreover, a govenment that eagerly consumes private capital through ever higher income and estate taxation, displaying an insatiable appetite for funds, cannot be expected for long to limit itself to the traditional sources. When government revenues begin to decline or fall short of projected needs, the nonprofit sector itself may become a revenue target. Taxes may be levied and regulations imposed in order to guide, or promote the flow of philanthropic funds for politically desirable ends. Moreover, inflation, which is a governmental technique of deficit financing, may ravish the capital assets of non-profit organizations. In the end, hyperinflation, which is the climax towards which all inflations tend to gravitate, may consume most capital assets and reduce all philanthropic organizations to hollow shells.

And yet, the most popular way to protect the assets from the eroding effects of death taxation is to establish a charitable foundation. Thousands of foundations owe their origins

58

to the wish to avoid the substantial tax liabilities that fall on large estates. They are the current fad of wealthy people, because gifts of property to foundations are not subject to gift taxes, and bequests are exempt from estate and inheritance taxes. Foundations may serve to maintain control of a family-owned corporation upon death of a principal owner by avoiding the sale of the assets to pay estate and inheritance taxes. They may be endowed with non-voting stock, while the family retains control over the corporation through the voting stock.

A foundation may be the only method for a family to maintain control over a large enterprise. Surely, the great wealth of Henry Ford or John D. Rockefeller could not be passed to the next generation by way of a few thousand dollars annual exemption; only a charitable foundation could accomplish that. As inflation raises the dollar value of all family enterprises, we must expect more foundations to emerge in order to preserve family position and wealth.

Foundations are creatures of an ever-changing legal system. As legal and social instruments for applying private wealth to public purposes, they are subject to the hazards of policy changes. When public opinion disapproves of large family fortunes, private foundations cannot be expected to remain unscathed for long.

Evasion

Public opinion may want the "loopholes" closed and the "give-aways" ended, which means, it may want the government to seize more private wealth. But the potential victims cannot be expected to stand idly by when their economic accomplishments are to be seized and distributed. They will react with tax "avoidance" by ever new legal procedures and devices, and "evasion" by breaking the letter of the law. It is a proven principle of taxation that tax burden and evasion are directly proportional — the higher the rate of taxation, the higher the rate of evasion. As federal death duties impose the most confiscatory tax burdens, we must assume the highest evasion rate for death duties. The low revenue yield of federal estate and gift taxes, in spite of confiscatory rates, supports this conclusion.

A taxpayer who deliberately omits an item of taxable income from his return violates the law. Surely, the temptation is great when a tax declaration will lead to an irretrievable loss of more than one-half of total family wealth. A simple deletion may safeguard it when it is hidden in a Swiss bank account or Liechtenstein family foundation. The insignificant amount of gift tax revenue now causes us to wonder how many gifts of cash and valuable assets are made every year by parents to their children in violation of the law.

Gift and estate tax evasion is part and parcel of the "underground economy" where trade and commerce prosper without records and reports to accountants and tax collectors. In most parts of the world the underground harbors the most essential part of economic activity, feeding and clothing the people, sustaining human life. Without it, life in the Soviet Union, the Iron Curtain countries, and Third-World countries would be immeasurably more wretched and precarious than it is even today. In fact, if it were not for the underground economy and its thriving black markets, millions of people in those countries would probably perish from hunger and want.

In the United States the underground is a relatively new economic phenomenon that appeared together with confiscatory taxation, oppressive regulation and rampant inflation during the 1960's and 70's. When inflation soared to double-digit rates and lifted most workers into income-tax brackets that originally were meant to afflict the affluent, much economic activity went underground. But the American underground differs from that in communist and socialist countries in that it specializes in the preservation of personal wealth rather than the procurement of essential consumers' goods. The people of Poland or Zaire may go to the underground in search of a loaf of bread or a pound of meat. Americans may visit it in order to convert their savings into "treasure" that can be hidden from income tax and estate tax collectors and is likely to survive this age of inflation.

Estate-tax evasion, which probably dates back to the 1930's when the tax rates first reached their confiscatory levels, can be called the forerunner of the American underground economy. It is so simple to escape the estate-tax collector and preserve family wealth. And it is so common and natural that most evaders hardly feel guilty when, at death's door, they make expensive gifts to their sons and daughters and their children. Many law-abiding individuals who never in their lives defrauded anyone and who honestly and punctually met all their tax obligations, feel at ease with their consciences when, dividing their worldly treasures for the last time, they fail to inform the gift-tax collector. In preparation for transfer, productive wealth is liquidated and converted to "mobile" and "invisible" assets that can change hands undetectedly. A hand full of diamonds, a few gold coins, paintings and art objects may constitute great wealth for every generation.

Every year large amounts of productive capital are liquidated and converted to "invisible wealth" that passes from generation to generation. Usually the family business is not sold, merely some liquid capital is withdrawn and converted for transfer, leaving visible only that part of wealth that is tax exempt. Where the business lacks the liquid assets needed for transfer they are created through debt encumbrance.

Estate tax evasion is most difficult for farmers and ranchers who normally lack the necessary liquidity and are short of the income needed to sustain heavy mortgage indebtedness. Their difficulties in evading the tax incidence may explain their vocal opposition to the estate tax, which caused the U.S. Congress, in 1976, to permit valuation of farmland and other property used in a closely-held business on the basis of its *use* rather than fair market value. The law introduced complicated valuation formulas that reduce certain appaisals for federal estate tax purposes. The maximum reduction in fair market value of qualified real property was set at $500,000. The 1981 tax act raised it to $750,000 over the next three years. But the 1976 tax act also imposed "recapture taxes" in the event the qualified property is sold by the family or ceases to be employed in a qualified use within 15 years after the decedent's death. Failure by the heir or a member of his family to participate in the business operation for three years or more is treated as a cessation of qualified use, which sets off the imposition of recapture taxes.

Many estate tax evaders use valuable real goods for transfer purposes. Their demand for expensive jewelry, precious metals and art objects may explain their extraordinary rise in prices in recent years, which in turn encouraged ever more conversion of productive wealth into "invisible" transferable wealth. Many evaders who are leery of this avenue of escape use financial instruments with anonymous ownership. There are some $380 billion of state and municipal bearer bonds, some $300 billion of industrial bearer notes and bonds, some $180 billion of commercial paper, all of which may move from hand to hand without record or report. However, in contrast to hard objects and the municipals, the latter may leave a visible trail through their interest income that is subject to income taxation. Nevertheless, no one will ever know the extent of their use in silent wealth transfer from generation to generation.

Elimination of anonymous ownership of easily negotiable bonds was part of the 1982 tax act's attack on the underground economy. Starting January 1, 1983, new issues to the public, maturing in a year or more, must be in registered form. If corporations fail to record the owners they lose the deductions for interest paid and are subject to excise taxes. Securities sold abroad to foreigners are exempted from the rules.

The law obviously created new avenues of escape. American issuers of financial securities henceforth will place more bearer instruments abroad where they will be readily sold to investors of unknown nationalities. No one will ever know the number of Americans who will temporarily forget their nationality when they invest in bearer instruments abroad. Many frightened Americans already have hidden large parts of their wealth in Swiss bank vaults and numbered accounts where no one but the banker himself will ever know the identity of the owner. His savings are safe where the law and constitution guarantee their secrecy.

The strong demand for bearer instruments together with their future restrictions by the 1982 tax act should give rise to a price premium of bearer issues over registered issues. The premium will vary with changes in demand and supply. Government policies that increase the burden of death duties through inflation and other devices and that reduce the supply of bearer instruments facilitating estate-tax escapes will tend to raise the premium. Individual ingenuity in devising ever new avenues of escape will tend to lower it. In the coming years the premium will be an objective indicator of the enduring struggle between government eager to consume productive wealth and the creators of wealth who are determined to preserve it.[29]

[29]For a brilliant discussion of "black markets," which in times of price and wage controls comprise an important part of the underground economy, Cf. Gary North, *How You Can Profit from the Coming Price Controls,* American Bureau of Economic Research, Durham, N.C.

Chapter 8
INFLATION TRANSFERS WEALTH — TAX FREE

Inflation causes serious upheavals in the distribution of income and property. There are long-term contracts that need not be fulfilled until a later time. There are long-term debts that need not be settled until years later, long-term employment contracts that involve money payments over time. They all are exposed to inflation which shifts income and wealth from the creditors to the debtors. When debts are settled in depreciated money the creditors are losing the amount of depreciation; the debtors who are making payment in cheaper money are gaining this very amount. Inflation creates "unearned" income for debtors and inflicts undeserved losses on creditors.

It is a popular, although erroneous, belief that inflation affects only wealthy individuals because they are said to be the money lenders. This may have been true during the Middle Ages when economic wealth was concentrated with a few wealthy noblemen and merchants, while the masses of people were struggling for mere survival. But today, many millions of people are the creditors of life insurance companies, pension funds, savings banks, etc. Millions own government bonds and other money assets. They all are losing massive amounts to their debtors.

Inflation is the most devious and most destructive government policy ever devised. It is a "transfer" policy that impoverishes millions of hard-working Americans while it enriches all debtors, especially the government that is conducting the policy. And yet, inflation can be made to serve as a very effective tool of intentional transfer of income and wealth from one individual to another. In particular, *inflation can be used to transfer family wealth from one generation to another, and to protect this wealth from confiscatory taxation.*

As a parent, you would like to leave your worldly possessions to your children. You may want them to continue the family business, to own the family farm or ranch, or just enjoy the fruits of family efforts. But government covets and, through its tax collectors, may seize a big share of your family income and wealth. If you know the workings of inflation, you can easily and legally thwart the seizure by using inflation as a transfer agent.

You just need to imitate the U.S. Treasury which presently is selling debt instruments that are falling due in the year 2008. At a 10 percent annual inflation rate it will make final payments in U.S. dollars that will be worth less than one 1982 penny. You can do the same in your family finances. You make no taxable gifts and leave no estate, which would be taxed at devastating rates. But *you sell your assets to your children at today's market prices in exchange for long-term debt instruments*. That is to say, you become a family creditor and your children the debtors. Inflation now will shift your wealth, unmolested by income taxes, capital gains taxes, gift taxes or estate taxes, to your children. In a few years of double-digit inflation they will own free and clear all the property you sold.

As the government issues its depreciating bonds, so may your child give you a 20-year mortgage as security against his debt. Inflation gnaws indiscriminately at both bond and mortgage, and thereby enriches the debtor at the expense of the creditor. But while the U.S. Treasury bond issue is designed to deceive the buyer and consume productive capital, the mortgage loan given by parents to children is made to serve the noble purpose of family wealth transfer and capital preservation.

You sell a house, farm or business to your son for $1,000,000. He gives you an interest-bearing note secured by a mortgage, payable in a lump sum 20 years from the date of sale. Double-digit inflation will shrink the balloon mortgage to a negligible amount, and even depreciate your income tax on any interest you may receive and the capital gains tax you may owe 20 years hence.

The sale obviously exchanges real assets that are rising in value for dollar claims that are depreciating in value. If you should die soon after the sale, not much will be gained from the transfer. The dollar claims would be in your estate and be subject to estate taxation. But if you should depart this life just 5 years after the sale, the paper in your estate would have eroded during the interim. Inflation may have doubled the price of the assets in the possession of your children, and reduced the value of your paper by one-half. Estate taxes may still be levied on your paper; but they, too, are payable in minidollars. Most independent economists are convinced that in a rage of hyperinflation, the U.S. dollar will become utterly worthless before the turn of this century, perhaps before the end of this decade. If they should prove to be correct and you should leave the stage of life at this time, the dollar claims in your estate will be equally worthless. Your children own the family business free and clear. The death duties, if any, will be payable in worthless dollars, which will be the same dollars the U.S. Government will be using in settlement of its trillion-dollar debt.

Inflation works equally well as wealth-transfer agent if you sell your property to your children in exchange for a *family annuity*. An annuity is an allowance or income received in one or more payments annually, typically from family members, life insurance companies, retirement funds, and others. Annuities are for a stated time or for life. In early America they were the most popular legal device by which the old generation relinquished the farm, ranch or business in exchange for life-long payments or services by the younger generation. Their popularity has waned in recent years because the life insurance companies gradually took the place of the family and became their primary sellers. Inflation then impoverished the annuitants as creditors while it enriched the insurance companies as debtors. But it continues to be a very effective device that, with the help of inflation, transfers wealth from parents to children. In fact, it may be superior to the sale of property in exchange for long-term notes and mortgages. They remain in a deceased's estate and are subject to death duties; the straight life annuity ceases to exist in the moment of death, leaving no estate asset and no liability to children.

A "stepped up" annuity may add more flavor to the inflation-transfer process. The parent receives smaller payments at first, or none at all, and when he or she reaches a certain age, usually upon retirement, he or she receives larger annuity payments. But in the meantime inflation had ample opportunity to do its wealth transfer work.

An Idaho rancher with one thousand acres of choice land is beginning to wonder about his estate-tax problems. He is 60 years of age, his wife is 58. The fair market value of his ranch is $2 million. He may reject special use valuation as too dangerous because it may entail "recapture taxes." Instead, he decides to sell his ranch to his children in exchange for a joint-life-and-survivor stepped-up annuity with payments commencing at his 65th birthday and continuing until both their deaths.

It is rather simple to devise such a sale. All he needs to do is to contact several life insurance companies and invite their annuity offers in exchange for a $2 million single premium. He will select one and then invite his children to match the insurance company's offer. The children become legal owners upon exchange of deed and annuity, but regular payment begins only five years later. If the father wants to keep on ranching he must arrange a lease-back and make rental payments.

Annuity payments are income and therefore taxable under a complicated formula that distinguishes between simple return of the rancher's capital, his capital gain, and the interest from both. All payments cease upon death of the last spouse. There is no wealth transfer at death, no estate, and therefore no tax. After all, there was a sale in exchange for an annuity that yielded a taxable income. Government collected its share through taxation of income and capital gains in the regular annuity payments.

Inflation is the driving force that pushes more and more estates into the jaws of confiscatory estate taxation. But it also opens many avenues of escape for astute observers who are ever mindful of the dangers. To avoid the dreaded inflation push *the value of the estate needs to be reduced or at least be frozen at present levels and all inflation growth be siphoned out of the estate.*

A businessman, farmer or rancher may form a limited partnership with his children of legal age. Such a partnership must contain at least one member whose liability is general and unlimited, hence called the "general" partner, and the member or members whose liability is limited to the capital invested. Although there are substantial differences, the limited partner's position resembles that of a lender whose return is narrowly limited and therefore also the value of his investment. In a limited partnership that aims at siphoning inflation growth from an estate to its heirs, the children are the general partners and the parents are the limited partners. Our two-million dollar rancher is the limited partner, his children are the general partners. He contributes $2 million to the partnership, his two children $10,000 each. Rampant inflation now raises the fair market price of the ranch to $4 million. As limited partner he still is worth $2 million, but his children as general partners also own $2 million, or one-half of the ranch. A few more years of inflation may lift the value of the ranch to $10 million of which $2 million belong to the rancher and $8 million to his children. The limited partnership froze the rancher's net worth and permitted inflation to shift family wealth to his children — tax free.

Some businessmen use a corporation to transfer income and wealth to their children. They may organize or reorganize a family business in such a way that their share of the business is frozen and all inflation growth accrues to their children. They may retain the preferred stock having a fixed dollar value and give their heirs the equity interest common stock, that is growing in value. Their preferred stock may be voting preferred, which preserves their control over the business and assures adequate executive income, but inflation is giving their children the substance of family wealth tax free.

An example of such siphoning is similar to that of the rancher. Two children who may be babies in their mother's arms receive a tax-exempt gift of $10,000 in common stock. The parents own the voting preferred stock worth $2 million. Rampant inflation conducted by a spendthrift administration now doubles the value of the business, which leaves $2 million to the parents and $2 million to the children now in kindergarten. Hyperinflation in the 1990's lifts the value of the business to $10 million or more, which leaves $2 million to the parents and $8 million or more to the children in 6th and 7th grades. Inflation silently and efficiently shifted the lion's share of family wealth to the children tax free.

If such a family organization is impractical, the estate owner may use a "holding company" i.e., a company controlling partial or complete interest in other companies, to achieve a similar transfer. He transfers his wealth to a corporation in which he acquires voting preferred stock of fixed dollar value, while the heirs subscribe to the equity stock at the residual value. Any growth in asset value then accrues to the heirs.

The owner may use the same principles by designing trusts under a will. To create a "siphoning" trust, he puts the marital deduction for the surviving spouse in one trust, and the balance of the estate that goes to the heirs in another. Fixed value assets are put in the former, while the equity assets promising either real or inflationary growth, are allocated to the latter. Any appreciation in estate value goes to its remaindermen.

The proper use of inflation as a wealth transfer agent permits the preservation of family wealth, which is a most desirable objective. After all, the family, which is antecedent to society, is the spring from which human effort and achievement flow. Financial destruction of the family through estate taxation or any other political means must have incalculable effects on society. To preserve the family and its achievement is a noble task.

Chapter 9
ON TRUSTS AND TRUST FUNDS

With the enactment of federal income and estate tax legislation, wealthy families sought devices that would minimize their tax burdens. For a while the trust appeared to offer a haven or refuge. But strenuous efforts on the part of government to block all routes to tax savings have greatly reduced the value of trusts as tax-saving devices. Numerous tax-reform acts have sought to "close the loopholes" through which productive family wealth could escape confiscation and consumption. Today, it is hard to conceive of a trust that is not beleaguered by laborious regulation, onerous income taxation, and federal estate or gift tax exactions.

The trust is an ancient institution through which one party administers property for the benefit of another. It comprises four essential elements: the *creator*, also called the donor, grantor, settlor, trustor; the *trustee*, who holds title to the property; the *beneficiary*, for whose benefit the property is held; and the *property* itself. Anyone who is legally capable of owning property can establish a trust, and anyone who is legally competent can act as trustee. A corporation cannot act as trustee unless its charter so stipulates. Most trusts are held and administered by qualified banks and trust companies.

Most trusts serve to protect inexperienced and incompetent individuals against loss of funds through bad investments. In connection with estate planning they aim to provide for the support of widows, minor children and dependents. Grantors place their wealth with a trustee for safekeeping and management instead of turning it over to a widow or to children inexperienced in business and investments. Trusts may be classified as to *time* when they take effect (testamentary trusts, living trusts), as to *activity* (active trusts, passive trusts such as life insurance trusts or land trusts), as to *revocability* (revocable and irrevocable trusts), as to *duration* (perpetual trusts, trusts for life, trusts for a term of years). One of the most popular trusts, because it may exist in perpetuity, has been the *public* or *charitable* trust, which serves the physical, mental or spiritual improvement of society.

The essence of trust is probably as old as man himself and his concern for his fellowman. But an urgent need for professional trustees and trust companies began to be felt only when the private property order of the last two centuries led to the formation and accumulation of productive capital that needed to be managed and safeguarded. The existence of personal wealth and the complexity of investment in the capitalistic world created a need for trust services.

Until the dawn of the transfer state these services could be rendered with ability and integrity. But in our age of inflation and regulation, trusts have ceased to function as dependable depositories of personal wealth. *To seek refuge in a trust holding monetary assets is like seeking protection in a fallout shelter without a roof.*

Of all the dangers to the wealth lodged in trusts, none is greater than inflation. It erodes the capital of all private and public trusts, charitable institutions, religious societies, scientific or literary foundations, and endowed colleges and universities. The depreciation of public and private debt and the fall of securities in terms of both price and purchasing power strike devastating blows not only at millions of small investors but also at all trusts managed by professional trustees and trust companies. Inflation ravishes the trust assets and impoverishes the beneficiaries.

The fate that has befallen the bond market in recent years may illustrate the point. With U.S. Treasury obligations selling at some 62 percent of par value (7 5/8s of Feb. 2002) and ATT issues (7s of 2001) at 55, all bond portfolios suffer from anemic depression. The capital assets of a private trust in Ohio, which we had an opportunity to examine in recent months, had lost some 12 percent in price between 1967 and 1981, and another 67 percent in value due to a 67 percent loss of U.S. dollar purchasing power, for a total loss of some 73 percent. Most trusts have lost more than 12 percent in price as bond prices plunged when interest rates soared to lofty levels. While they are bemoaning the elevated level of interest rates and low bond prices, they like to ignore the staggering losses in dollar purchasing power, which may be invisible but are all the more painful.

Asset managers who specialize in blue-chip stock portfolios like to ignore this loss in dollar purchasing power.

71

They are watching and competing with the Dow Jones averages or the Standard & Poor's 500 indicator, or the Value Line Index. But no one is recalculating his performance in terms of yesteryear's dollars. Such a calculation would be too depressing for trustees and beneficiaries alike. It would reveal that a blue-chip stock portfolio that kept up with the Dow Jones industrial average (now 840) lost 23.6 percent in price since 1965 and 70 percent in purchasing power, for a total loss of 78 percent of the original asset value. In short, the average stock investor fared even more poorly than the bond investor who sought safety rather than growth.

It is difficult to estimate the total losses suffered by the trusts as a result of the dollar depreciation. But our calculation, together with actual examinations of foundation assets, lead us to estimate the total losses of older institutions that were exposed to the dollar inflation of the last 15 years, to approach 80 percent. We need not elaborate the economic and social consequences of such losses.

Where trust institutions had the freedom, foresight, and financial know-how to seek shelter from the inflation ravages, the results were less destructive. While inflation inflicts havoc on monetary instruments it has varied effects on the value of real estate. Agricultural land, on the whole, survives periods of feverish inflation rather well as the prices of agricultural products tend to keep up with the inflation rates. Similarly, industrial and commercial property prices tend to adjust to inflation, although they may move erratically and wildly in reaction to the boom and bust cycles that accompany the inflation.

It is a sad fact that few trustees, if any, actually succeeded in sheltering their funds through proper investments. The reason for the dismal failure of nearly every trustee must be sought in a combination of restraints and limitations that, in the end, tend to be ruinous to all personal wealth.

It is the legal duty of a trustee to secure the maximum safety for his trust and, at the same time, a reasonable income. He must shun speculation and investment for the purpose of appreciation and gain. To assure prudent management the courts of several states have limited trust investments to a very small number of permitted securities, such as government bonds and first mortgages on real estate.

It is difficult to concoct a more ruinous investment program than that devised by these courts. While the U.S. dollar fell to 10¢ of its 1933 value and interest rates rose from 4 percent to 18 percent, which caused all such debt instruments to crash, the courts, in the name of prudence, ordered trust investment in those securities only. The judges, refusing to see the wrongful consequences of inflation, steadfastly ruled, and continue to rule, that the 1933 gold dollar is the same as the 1982 paper mini-dollar and that trust beneficiaries are properly served with shrinking mini-dollars.

In several states the legislature adopted lists of classes of securities, but not particular investments, in which a trustee is permitted or required to invest. It is rather easy to guess the composition of a trust list prepared by politicians assembled in legislature. Without fail, at the top of the list are their own state obligations, state bonds, notes and bills, obligations of municipalities, school districts, sewer districts, etc., etc. They, too, were subject to the ravages of rampant inflation and soaring interest rates, which reduced their value in terms of purchasing power to small fractions of their original value. In those states the trust beneficiaries are as poor and wretched today as they are in states where they were guarded by judges.

In most states the courts or legislatures established the so-called "prudent man rule" under which a trustee is protected in managing investments if he uses the skill and care of a reasonably prudent man. This rule affords greater flexibility in making adjustments to changing conditions. It permits trustees to invest a reasonable proportion of assets in common and preferred stocks that have shown satisfactory performance in recent years.

Even if such trust investments are made in common and preferred stock the net result rarely differs from that of the other systems. A preferred stock is no more inflation-resistant than a bond or mortgage. It depreciates at the inflation rate. And common stock investments, as measured by the indices, have performed as poorly during the last 17 years as have authorized debt instruments. The exceptional trustee may occasionally discover and invest in an exceptional growth stock allowed under the "prudent-man" rule.

He may even earn a profit that will reduce the losses suffered in other portions of the trust portfolio and from currency depreciation. But it is doubtful that his total fund is escaping grievous losses.

To the casual observer, the staggering losses suffered by personal trusts or corporate trusts holding employee profit-sharing and pension funds, are rarely visible. After all, the trustee who is holding and investing the funds is not calculating in *constant* dollars that would reveal the inflation losses, but in current dollars that are more appealing to the eye and yet so calamitous to the property.

Only a small proportion of the trust companies that administer trusts and estates concentrate upon this service. Most trust companies are also banks — commercial and savings banks with state or federal charters. Being creatures of the state, the former are under the supervision of and subject to examination by the state banking authorities. The trust departments of national banks are under the supervision of the Comptroller of the Currency and the Federal Reserve Board. All these government authorities are eagerly enforcing the trust rules.

Most trusts are administered by qualified banks and trust companies earning fees and commissions for their services and employing numerous trust officers. And yet, their record in the performance of fiduciary tasks has been notoriously poor. Their freedom of action is narrowly circumscribed by the government authorities that examine them or by the courts that appoint them. They have no choice but to invest heavily in government bonds and notes which, according to one eminent economist, are "certificates of guaranteed expropriation." No one can dispute that they have lost 90 percent of their value in just one generation and continue to lose purchasing power every day.

To observe a banker in his performance of fiduciary duties is rather painful even to a disinterested bystander. Having taken physical possession of and received title to all assets designated for the trust, he may proceed to liquidate all hard assets, such as real estate, gold and silver, and other valuables and replace them with trust assets, that is, eligible debt instruments and approved preferred and common stock. He may weed out of any given stock portfolio the "speculative" issues that would not pass government inspection. In short, he may diligently open the trust gates to the ravages of inflation and get paid handsomely for his efforts.

When the law permitted banks and trust companies to invest in precious metals, scarcely any availed themselves of this opportunity. They were legally free, between 1975 to 1981, to invest in the only natural money, the money of the ages, in man's most guarded treasure, in wealth that may change hands but is never consumed — in gold. But bankers no longer are thinking of the nature of man and of inexorable economic laws or principles. After half a century of meticulous government supervision and political paper money, they are thinking and acting like civil servants who are ever obedient and eager to please the authorities.[30]

Similar criticism can be levelled at most attorneys-at-law and other members of the legal profession. As a professional group they are influential and their voices are heard in government. And yet, they are keeping conveniently silent about the political destruction of money and moneyed wealth. After all, they are trained to think and act in terms of man-made law duly enacted and enforced; the inexorable laws of human action are utterly alien to them.

Attorneys are engaged in a public calling and therefore are officers of the court. They give skilled legal and tax advice, which may reduce tax liabilities or even eliminate them entirely. They devise and create a large variety of complicated trusts, most of which are like fallout shelters without a roof. Ignoring the ruinous consequences of inflation, they write wills and create trusts that make their beneficiaries the primary victims of inflation. They deliver their clients to banks, trust companies and other money managers, where family wealth is tossed in the maelstrom of inflation.

Few attorneys are mindful of monetary depreciation. Those who are aware of inflation and its consequences may recommend "revocable living trusts" as a principal estate planning device that permits the grantor to act also as the trustee of the trust. Husband or wife, or both, may create a

---

[30]It is ironic that the Economic Recovery Tax Act of 1981 rescinded the freedom to invest trust and pension funds in gold. The Act meant to promote the demand for eligible trust paper, preferably government securities, permitting government to spend and borrow more at lower interest rates. The Tax Equity and Fiscal Responsibility Act of 1982 did not restore the freedom.

trust with one or both as trustees. The trust is revocable and amendable as long as both continue to live. Upon the death of one partner, the surviving spouse as trustee can buy, sell, and manage the property without limitation. She has unlimited use of the income until her death when the property passes to the designated beneficiaries or those persons named by her. The Living Trust does not deliver her to a trust department, but may achieve substantial savings of federal estate tax. If one spouse becomes incompetent due to age or illness, the other assumes control. If both should fail to function, a successor trustee can step into the trusteeship and pay all bills and make all investments. The Living Trust may effectively avoid lengthy and costly probate procedures. But above all, it may hold family businesses, professional corporations, small business corporations in which undistributed income is taxable to its shareholders (Subchapter "S" Stock), and hard assets such as antiques, works of art, gold, silver, diamonds, etc. In short, it may be a shelter with a roof skillfully designed and properly constructed.[31]

Most trusts continue to inflict undue anguish and pain on the beneficiaries, especially on the widow. After her husband's death, she discovers to her greatest dismay that she has lost control of her own life. The family wealth is transferred to a trustee banker who handles her money as if it were his. While he is doling out her rations like Ebenezer Scrooge, he is generous with his own fees and expenses and tragically oblivious to the dangers of inflation. What husband and wife have created together a trust can tear apart.

---

[31]Cf. B. Ray Anderson, *Inflation Tax Planning*, Anderson-Nearon, Inc., Walnut Creek, Palo Alto, Los Angeles and Newport Beach, California, pp. 36-37.

Chapter 10
ALTERNATIVES AND REFORM PROPOSALS

Article I, Section 8, of the Constitution stipulates that "Congress shall have power to lay and collect taxes." The President can make recommendations, but only Congress can translate them into law. Congress may adopt, revise, or even reject Presidential tax proposals and proceed on its own. Behind this great constitutional authority of Congress stands the ultimate power of all democratic processes: public opinion. It is public opinion that in regular elections determines the political and ideological composition of Congress, which in turn affects and guides its votes. In a democratic society no basic policy, especially no tax measure, can be pursued for long without the approval and support of the public. Under great pressures from political forces and economic and social groups, Congress tends to reflect the hopes and aspirations of the public.

The Committee on Ways and Means of the House of Representatives, the most powerful committee in the House, is the focal point for all matters of public finance. In its public hearings, public opinion comes to the fore in its personalities, pressures, forces, and conflicts. Individuals who appear before the Committee usually represent a cross-section of opinion. They are hurling a mass of information at the Committee, while its members are besieged by their own constituents seeking changes in the tax bill.

A society that seeks reformation and redistribution needs vast appropriations of money. The search for money, and more money, is a chronic symptom of the policy of redistribution. Its beneficiaries and their advocates can be expected to plead for ever higher levies and benefits, while its victims, from whom the transfer means are extracted, are pleading their cases for tax relief. The debate between both groups affords an excellent insight into the aspirations and values of the American public.

Even the reformers and equalizers are admitting that estate and gift taxes are disappointing in revenue and have little effect on the distribution of wealth. The rates may be high enough, they assert, but there are too many ways to escape, too many "loopholes" that need to be closed, e.g., the marital deduction, the freedom to make gifts during lifetime, generation-skipping trusts and outright transfers, charitable foundations, etc. The public is just too apathetic and ignorant about the merits of property transfer taxes.[32]

As an alternative to the estate tax, which concentrates on the gross estate of the testator, the federal government conceivably could concentrate on the person who receives the bequest and levy an *inheritance* tax on him. All states, except Nevada, have long, unsatisfactory experiences with such a duty which yields even less than estate taxation.[33] When an estate is divided into many shares, each recipient is taxed at lower bracket rates. Large estates could conceivably escape untaxed if the number of recipients is great enough and their shares small enough for each recipient to qualify for annual exclusion. Furthermore, when each gift or bequest is taxed separately the recipient of many small inheritances pay lower taxes than the recipient of a lump sum, which is unequal taxation from the same inheritance.

Such deficiencies, together with the states' great reluctance to surrender their traditional source of revenue, have discouraged the federal government from devising federal inheritance duties. But they have given rise to demands for a new tax — the *accessions* tax — which is a modification of the inheritance tax principle. It is a progressive, cumulative tax on an individual's lifetime receipts of gifts and inheritances. Each new acquisition would be taxed progressively after computation of all earlier acquisitions. It has great appeal to those who seek a more equal distribution of wealth because the steep progression of rates would tend to hold down the total wealth received by any one individual. But to the dismay of its sponsors the accessions tax admittedly would yield even less than estate and inheritance taxation, and would offer many opportunities for avoidance through discretionary trusts, foundations, and other legal devices.[34]

All such alternatives do not differ materially from those reform proposals that seek to close one more loophole or

---

[32] Joseph A. Pechman, *op. cit.*, p. 210
[33] Shultz and Harris, *ibid.*, p. 498.
[34] Joseph A. Pechman, *ibid.*, pp. 208, 209.

block one more avenue of escape to make the levy more productive. The equalizers' faith in the tax object is equaled only by their trust in this next step that is supposed to achieve the desired objective. But if it should fail again because the wicked men of wealth are known to devise ever new ways of escape, they surely will return, with faith undaunted, to demand ever stricter measures of confinement and expropriation. And again, they will intone the sounds of liberty, equality and justice while building another roadblock for those Americans who happen to travel that road.

Closing the Loopholes

Government spokesmen can always be expected to present a fiscal case for higher revenue — unless public opinion strongly favors tax relief. After all, public opinion can be translated into political votes, which may mean victory or defeat in the next election. While in office, *Secretary of the Treasury, William E. Simon,* yielded to the pressures for an increase in the estate tax exemption, but immediately wanted to abolish the lower bracket tax rates on the first $90,000 of taxable estate. For the sake of a "smoother rate progression" he would tax all taxable estates at rates ranging from 30 percent to 77 percent, instead of just 3 percent to 77 percent which is in effect today. In his own words:

We believe that an increase in the estate tax exemption is clearly warranted. Indeed, such an increase is essential if the estate tax is to be returned to its historic role as an excise on the transfer of relatively larger wealth accumulations. At the same time we cannot ignore the significant revenue consequences that would result from increasing the estate tax exemption. Thus, we recommend that the estate tax exemption be increased to $150,000 over a 5-year transition period and that the lower bracket estate tax rates on the first $90,000 of taxable estate be eliminated. Limiting the increase to $150,000 (with the proposed rate changes) will permit the revenue loss to be held to an acceptable amount, which can be absorbed gradually during the phase-in period.[35]

William E. Simon yielded to public opinion for liberalized payment provisions for family farms and businesses. But while he agreed to a 5-year moratorium, 20-year extended

[35]*Ibid.*, March 23, 1976, p. 4.

payment provisions, and an interest reduction from 7 percent to 4 percent on delayed tax payments, he would limit these concessions to the first $300,000 of taxable estates. No concession was to be made to larger concentrations of wealth.[36]

The Secretary readily yielded to the charge that the federal estate tax is a widow tax. Therefore, he recommended "the adoption of a free interspousal transfer rule, or unlimited marital deduction, under which all transfers between spouses would be completely excluded from the estate and gift taxes. Such a rule best comports with the way most couples manage their property and would substantially simplify the estate tax law and the administration of estates."[37] But he wanted to see the new transfer rule postponed for revenue reasons, until such times when he would no longer be in office. And yet, we must respect the Secretary for his strong stand against those forces that promise an increased estate tax exemption and then would raise death tax burdens through a new tax on unrealized appreciation in property transferred at death. His opposition to such schemes advanced by the American Bankers Association appeals especially to millions of owners of farms and small businesses who would be the primary victims of the new tax. In the words of the Secretary:

> We oppose these proposals to change the present treatment of unrealized appreciation in property transferred at death. We are unable to discern any consistent rationale underlying such proposals other than a desire to increase death taxes; and we believe that decisions regarding the proper level of death taxes should be made through a review of estate and gift tax rates and exemptions, rather than through the device of tax on appreciation in an estate. Moreover, the pressing need today is for estate tax relief rather than an increase in death tax burdens. It would be wholly inappropriate to hold forth the promise of such relief through an increased estate tax exemption and then to make that promise illusory through a tax on unrealized appreciation that will fall

---

[36]*Ibid.*, pp. 8, 9.
[37]*Ibid.*, p. 10. His proposal was made law by the Economic Recovery Tax Act of 1981 and became effective in 1982.

particularly heavily on the owners of farms and small businesses.[38]

The sway of an ideology over the minds of the people is said to be complete when the victims themselves join in the public chorus that is singing its praises. The sway of the new morality that seeks economic and social equality by political force is surely complete when the *American Bankers Association,* which consists of some 14,000 banks of whom 4,000 exercise fiduciary powers as trustees and executors, joins in the clamor for higher estate taxation. In fact, the Association is proposing the imposition of a new tax, "an additional, or appreciation, estate tax (AET) on net appreciation in a decedent's estate." It is true, the Association favors a token adjustment of the estate tax exemption to $100,000, which does not nearly compensate for the inflationary erosion in recent years, but then would reduce it again by any part of the $30,000 gift tax exemption that is used. And it favors lowering the estate tax rates, particularly in the $100,000 to $500,000 range. But then it urges, upon certain conditions, that a transfer tax be imposed upon the termination of a limited trust interest, that great grandchildren be denied tax considerations as members of family, that property transfers during life be added to the estate, which then can be taxed at higher rates.[39]

Even the Secretary of the Treasury, who *ex officio* is no champion of lower taxes, seemed aghast at the ABA position. In his statement to the Committee he commented on the ABA proposal.

When the rhetoric is cut away, the AET proposal gives credence to what many of us have long suspected; proposals to tax capital gains at death are not fundamentally grounded in income tax concerns but are essentially an effort to increase death tax burdens. That being the case, the threshold question is whether those burdens should be increased. In our view they should not be increased. Indeed the extent of the present burden has become so severe that the Administration has recommended meas-

---

[38]*Ibid.,* p. 17.

[39]*Ibid.,* March 15, 1976, pp. 26-283. The Tax Reform Act of 1976 adopted the ABA proposal and unified the estate and gift taxes, so that a single progressive rate schedule was applied to cumulative gifts and bequests. The Economic Recovery Tax Act of 1981 retained this provision.

ures to alleviate the burden by increasing the exemption and providing for a deferral of payment of tax in certain situations.

Our judgment of the ABA position is more comprehensive than that of the Secretary. If the 257-page statement actually reflects the economic and social thinking of American bankers, we cannot escape from drawing the most dire conclusions. If our bankers, who are the professional guardians of the people's savings and capital markets, blithely ignore the devastating losses suffered from inflation and taxation, the policy of capital consumption and destruction must continue unchecked. In the end, a flood of hyperinflation and confiscatory taxation will inundate and bankrupt the industry that was already bankrupt intellectually and morally.

The American Bankers Association is enjoying the company of many other organizations that are pressing for higher death duties. The *Public Citizen Tax Reform Research Group* is building its case on the contradistinction between "earned" income and "inherited" income. "We have a choice," its spokesmen conclude, "of whether to shift even greater burdens on the people's work incentives through social security and income taxes . . . or taxing the amount which adults can inherit from their parents. Given the choices, this committee should be looking for ways to increase estate and gift tax revenues."[40] "Earned income" by working people who labor bravely under heavy taxation is depicted in sympathetic colors. But inherited income of "the millionaires" is a windfall that mostly escapes estate and gift taxes — "our most neglected taxes." In short, fallacious economic arguments are reinforced by insidious appeals to resentment and envy.

The *American Institute of Certified Public Accountants,* our experts on profits and losses, partially agrees with the "Research Group" although it lacks the Group's loud ideological color. It designed and proposed a new tax that is to correct a glaring oversight in the present tax laws. "Under current law," the accountants argue,

an individual can transfer property (by gift or bequest) to a person two or more generations removed and, so long as an intervening generation is limited to an income inter-

---

[40] *Ibid.*, p. 394.

est, no estate or gift tax is imposed on the intervening generation. This has been characterized as an abuse since it does permit transfer of property for the benefit of several generations without taxing each level. Our position is that there should be a tax upon transfers in trust with an income interest to an intervening generation, but we favor the approach of imposing the tax on the estate of the intervening generation, rather than on the testator or settlor.[41]

The accountants would also unify the two systems of transfer taxes, estate and gift taxes, in order to include 75 percent of the fair market value of *inter vivos* gifts in the estate tax computation. It would put all estates from which gifts have been made into higher tax brackets.[42]

Many tax attorneys and public finance economists are members of a taxpayers' lobby, called *Taxation with Representation*. This group presents its plea for higher taxes under such colorful ideological labels as "curbing the emergence of a self-perpetuating aristocracy of wealth whose goals and outlook are incompatible with democratic ideals."[43] Of course, the attorneys neglect to offer proof that their opponents intentionally or unwittingly support the emergence of a self-perpetuating aristocracy of wealth. Well-versed in the tricks of debate they deduce their conclusions from unproven assertions, or use colorful adjectives or nouns that already contain the conclusions. For instance, without any proof whatever, the lobby asserts that the new taxes it proposes, such as a surtax on generation-skipping transfers and taxation of capital gains at death or gift, help to make up for the "deficiencies of our loophole-ridden income tax," by insuring that wealth — including that "accumulated through manipulation of income tax loopholes" — nevertheless bears some federal tax at least once a generation.[44]

Senator Edward M. Kennedy of Massachusetts, an impor-

---

[41]*Ibid.*, p. 287. The Tax Reform Act of 1976 imposed a "Generation-Skipping Transfer Tax; but exempted wills and revocable trusts under certain conditions.

[42]*Ibid.*, p. 294. The Tax Reform Act of 1976 adopted the proposal by including 100 percent of the fair market value of gifts in the estate tax computation.

[43]*Ibid.* March 16, 1976, p. 67.

[44]*Ibid.*

tant ideological leader on the American political scene, outlined his view in a letter to Congressman Al Ullman, Chairman of the House Ways and Means Committee (released by the office of the Senator, March 15, 1976). Although the Senator does not present his statement in the glaring ideological colors of the tax attorneys, he, too, endeavors to reinforce his case with political oratory: "Reforms are necessary to insure that an estate and gift tax system is both fair and effective in achieving its objectives." He is recommending "revision of the rate structure to distribute the tax burden in a more equitable manner." Unfortunately, he does not tell us how the system could be made fairer and the rates more equitable, and why previous legislation was so unfair and inequitable. But his letter leaves no doubt that he would like to broaden the tax and make it more effective in preventing "undue concentration of wealth." In his own words:

I believe that the Congress should reject out of hand proposals such as those advanced by President Ford to increase the present $60,000 estate tax exemption to a level of $150,000 or even $200,000 as suggested by others. Such a proposal would virtually eliminate the federal estate tax as an effective federal revenue measure and as a means of insuring that undue concentrations of wealth are not perpetuated in the United States. Increasing the federal estate tax exemption level to $200,000, for example, would cut by almost one-half the revenues presently obtained from the federal estate tax.

The ultimate thrust of tax reform should be to broaden the scope of the estate tax, not restrict it. To employ an increase in the estate tax exemption to solve liquidity problems of deceased farmers is to let the tail wag the dog. The benefits of increasing the excemption to $150,000 or $200,000 would extend far beyond those owning farms, and would provide estate tax reductions in situations in which it is neither needed nor desirable. The Federal estate tax must not be gutted under the guise of providing assistance to owners of family farms.

The Senator makes two specific proposals that deserve our attention. In complete agreement with the tax attorneys he would like to insure that "transfers of wealth are taxed at least once each generation, thus eliminating the generation-skipping transfers that now allow wealthy families to avoid estate taxes for as much as 100 years." The tax that began as an emergency levy on property transfers, which then was made an instrument for equalization of wealth upon occasion of transfer, now is to be levied more often. The Senator's arbitrary proposal of at least one imposition each generation may soon be followed by other proposals to levy the tax once every ten years, or five years, or every year. After all, in an exchange system, like ours, personal property changes hands more often than once every generation. Why should anyone who chooses not to transfer his property escape the transfer tax?

His most interesting reform proposal refers to family farms. The Senator proposes to value farm land at its value for farm use, provided that the following conditions are met: The decedent in his or her will, or the decedent's estate within the period of time for filing a federal estate tax return, transfers the *development rights* with respect to the property to a state or local government, to the Secretary of Agriculture, or a charitable organization. Such transfers would satisfy the federal estate tax liability that is attributable to the difference between the market price of the land and the farm use value.

According to the Senator:

"development rights" are actually negative easements. they do not give the holder of the rights the power to take any action with respect to the land covered by the development rights, except the right to prevent commercial or residential development of the land. Thus, for example, the use of the farm property as farm property by the heirs and beneficiaries of the decedent will not in any way be impaired by possession of the development rights by a state or local government.

This proposal will insure that federal estate taxes will be forgiven only in those situations in which there is assurance that the farm property will in fact continue to be used as farm property. If at some later date, the owners of the farm desire to develop the land, or to sell it to a purchaser who wishes to develop the land, the owners can do so and they (or the purchaser) may acquire the development rights from the State or local government, charitable organization, or the Secretary of Agriculture, as the case may be, by paying to the holder of the rights the current fair market value of the rights. (*Ibid.*, p. 3)

The Senator obviously is holding the farmers' intelligence in low regard. To avoid the estate tax, which for most farmers may amount to 10, 20, or 30 percent of the farm value, they may transfer 100 percent of the development value, which may be a multiple of the former. To save $1 the Senator urges them to give away $4, and potentially much more. But if he should change his mind, the farmer may buy back the development rights at the "current fair market value." That is, he may save the tax on the development value, but later may repurchase the full development value from government or foundation. If oil should be discovered on his land, he may repurchase the oil deposit at fair market value.

The Senator's proposal may raise yet other questions in the minds of farmers. Once government owns the development rights, will it not be tempted to use these rights "for the common good," i.e., as government sees fit? And would it not be tempted to refuse the resale of the rights to the farmer who can afford to repurchase them, but may want to develop the land in an "unauthorized" manner?

Neither tax attorneys nor tax accountants, not even some politicians, can be as blunt and thoroughgoing as university professors with tenure. After all, they need not be concerned with clients they must please, nor even with votes they need for re-election. *Professor Gerard M. Brannon*, professor of economics at Georgetown University, illustrates the case when he furiously flails at President Ford for having proposed tax changes with which he disagrees. "Kick him in the teeth," that, according to the professor, is President Ford's proposal for dealing with "some hard-working poor boy who wants to own a farm." To defer payment of death duties is making a loan to rich people, which is vicious tax policy. To the professor "the thrust of President Ford's proposals to defer estate tax on family farms and family business is basically a scheme to make interest-free loans to rich people."[45]

---

[45]*Hearings*, March 16, 1976, p. 224. Cf. also Professors Carl S. Shoup, *Ibid.*, March 23, 1976, pp. 70-76; Michael J. Graetz, pp. 77-91; James Smith, pp. 109-139; Edward C. Halbach, pp. 140-147; and Gerald R. Jantscher of the Brookings Institution, pp. 148-158.

Professor Brannon's furious case for substantive estate tax reform reads like a summary of all those proposals that would increase the death duties. He would close the "major loopholes," tax unrealized appreciation at death, raise gift tax rates to the estate tax level, include gifts in the estate tax base, and impose an extra tax on generation-skipping transfers, all in order to achieve his ultimate objective: greater economic equality. But no matter how warped and desultory his case may be, it deserves our attention because of its peculiar philosophical rationale: to improve the capitalist system. He assures us: "We have a capitalist system and we need to make it work effectively. What makes capitalism work is the incentive to earn money. One of the disadvantages of capitalism is the extremes of wealth and poverty that it generates, which is why we have progressive taxes and poverty relief."[46]

This incentive to earn money obviously does not include the right to keep it; a steeply progressive income tax may claim the lion's share. And it does not include the right to bequeath savings to children; a progressive estate tax may claim most of them. Actually, highly progressive taxes narrowly encompass the incentive to earn money to average performance and productivity.

The most remarkable feature of this case for higher death duties is its utter unawareness of the functions of productive capital. The professor of economics does not once mention the term "capital," which designates a basic factor of production and constitutes a rudimentary subject of economic inquiry. "Capitalism," even in its original sense and meaning given by Karl Marx, denotes an economic and social system that is characterized by the employment of massive quantities of productive capital. Professor Brannon and many other reformers of his persuasion propose to improve and save capitalism through tax reforms that would consume capital, the very substance of the system.

Pleas for Tax Relief

Political observers agree that there is broad sentiment for estate tax reforms among Democrats and Republicans. But this can hardly be surprising in a society that is always in need of more funds for urgent social services and benefits,

---

[46]*Ibid.*, p. 225.

while its victims who must finance the services are pleading for tax relief. The ardent debate on estate taxation is merely a sideshow of an over-all tax reform controversy, especially on important elements of income and corporate tax changes.

It would be a grave mistake to assume that the tax victims are presenting their pleas from the lofty platform of moral indignation or resentment of a reform policy that aims at reshaping society. On the contrary, nearly all pleas for tax relief readily admit the philosophical presuppositions of progressive death duties as wealth equalizers and social reform. The numerous spokesmen for special exemptions and reductions appear before the committees of Congress like the convicted criminal who, before the judge passes sentence, is pleading for mercy. Most of them do not even point at the futility of the tax that is designed to foster economic equality, but actually lowers labor productivity and income, and thus promotes inequality. Nearly all their statements are made as special tax pleas that basically support the system of progressive taxation. "Let us tax the rich, but I am not one of them," is the loudest plea for reform.

Allan Grant of the *American Farm Bureau Federation*, which is the largest general farm organization with a membership of 2,505,258, urges the Congress to readjust the 1942 exemption of $60,000 to the depreciated purchasing power of the dollar of today, which would allow for a $200,000 exemption. No mention is made of tomorrow's inflation, which may depreciate the dollar even further and may necessitate more pleas for readjustment in the future. Similarly, he urges readjustment of the marital deduction without consideration of tomorrow's inflation and the need for more readjustments in the future.

The Farm Bureau's case is especially weak in its popular pleas for special valuation of land used for farming, woodland or scenic open space. Such land is to be taxed at its use value, and all other land at its market value. In other words, the steeply progressive rates of taxation are to be augmented by progressive rates of valuation. The progressive rates from 3 to 77 percent should be supplemented by progressive value rates from, let us say, 10 percent to 100 percent, depending on how the land is used, and on the discretion of the legislature that determines the ratio between market price and use value. That is, government will assume more discretionary powers to extend favors and privileges to favorite groups, and politicalize land values.

According to Allan Grant, these three changes are needed in the present federal estate tax law:

(1) Raise the specific estate tax exemption from $60,000 to $200,000. This would adjust the estate exemption for the inflation which has occurred since 1942, when the $60,000 exemption went into effect. (The consumer price index 1967 = 100 was 48.8 in 1942 and 161.2 in 1975. This means the purchasing power of $1.00 in 1975 was about equal to the purchasing power of 30 cents in 1942, and $60,000 divided by .30 equals $200,000).

(2) Raise the maximum marital deduction from 50 percent of the value of the adjusted gross estate passed to a surviving spouse to $100,000 plus 50 percent of the total value of the adjusted gross estate. This would recognize the importance of partnerships between husbands and wives, and the special problems of wives who are widowed at an early age.

(3) Establish a procedure which would permit the executor of an estate to elect to have land used for farming, woodland or scenic open space assessed for estate tax purposes on the basis of its current use rather than higher potential uses.[47]

Such special favor pleas, as made by the last point of the Farm Bureau program, always overlook the fact that everyone can avail himself of the favor. Rich people are well known for their acumen in seeking ever new opportunities for investments in durable assets that are taxed at lower rates. Surely they could be expected soon to concentrate on buying large tracts of farmland, woodland, and scenic open spaces in order to escape higher death duties. But in the hands of rich people such holdings would once again become "loopholes" that need to be closed. In the end, government would have to define precisely who could qualify for special

---

[47]*Ibid.*, March 15, 1976, p. 2. The Tax Reform Act of 1976 permitted valuation of certain property on the basis of its actual use, thereby producing a lower value for federal estate tax purposes. The Act also imposed post-death recapture taxes in the event the family sells the property within 15 years of the decedent's death or the property ceases to be employed for "qualifying uses." Special-use valuation was limited to $500,000.

valuation. Perhaps, it may need to license the owners of farmland, woodland and open spaces in a way they are licensed in totalitarian systems. The Farm Bureau then may find to its great dismay that many of its members do not qualify for the license, while many millionaires with better political connections and legal assistance are enjoying the special land valuation.

Nearly all farmers' associations are pleading for land valuation on the basis of current use rather than market price. To name just a few, there are the Midcontinent Farmers Association,[48] the Plains Cotton Growers, Inc., [49] the National Association of Wheat Growers,[50] the National Live Stock Commitee,[51] the American National Cattlemen's Association, [52] and the National Farmers Union.[53] They are strongly supported by forest owners and their associations, such as the Forest Industries Committee,[54] and the American Forestry Association.[55] The Maryland Historical Trust would like to apply the existing-use assessment principle also to all properties listed on the National Register of Historic Places.[56] And finally, the environmental and preservation groups concur with all of them on this issue. But they do not dare testify before a committee of Congress for fear of losing their tax-exempt status.

Senator Charles C. Mathias, Jr., of Maryland is one of their able spokesmen in the Congress. He introduces his case with a lucid description of a world of coming shortages, with hunger and want for millions of people:

Our resources and accomplishments have rightfully been, and will continue to be, a cause for great national pride and thanksgiving, but our natural resources are also rapidly becoming a cause for concern. The era of abundance has ended; increasing population and expectations put ever-increasing demands on the ability of man and nature to provide. Within the past decade we have

---

[48]*Ibid.*, p. 13.
[49]*Ibid.*, p. 18.
[50]*Ibid.*, p. 22.
[51]*Ibid.*, March 16, p. 186.
[52]*Ibid.*
[53]*Ibid.*, March 19, p. 8.
[54]*Ibid.*, March 16, p. 147.
[55]*Ibid.*, p. 154.
[56]*Ibid.*, March 19, p. 15.

been forced to recognize shortages in water, clean air and most recently, energy. Unfortunately, in each case we failed to heed the warning signs of impending shortage; we failed to take necessary actions, or even recognize the problems, before they became crises of major proportions ... The initial collision date of soaring population and food supply is fast approaching. The crisis this collision will create will dwarf the energy crisis — for it will not merely cause a loss of convenience, or even jobs, but mass starvation of millions of our fellow human beings.[57]

According to the Senator, we need to keep land in agricultural production. But all too often, farmers must sell their land to developers or speculators to pay their taxes. Therefore, tax laws and IRS policy must be changed lest they drive ever more farmers off their land. The Senator is proud of having introduced Senate bill 80 to eliminate "these confiscatory tax policies" by granting the option of having the decedent's interest in farmland, woodland, or open spaces determined by its use value rather than its fair market value.

How does an estate qualify for the special valuation? The property must have been devoted to one of these uses for a period of 5 years preceding the death of the decedent. But if the land should later

be converted to a non-qualifying use or even rezoned to permit a non-qualifying use for a period of ten years after the death giving rise to the estate tax, then the excess of the tax liability based on market valuation over liability based on qualifying use must be paid, plus 9 percent interest ... These stiff recapture provisions are necessary to prevent abuses and loopholes; it must be made impossible for the lower tax assessment to be afforded to 'phony' farmland already slated for development or which is developed after the estate tax is assessed. Windfall to speculators should be the last thing that should occur.[58]

He estimates that his bill will grant some $20 million in tax relief to qualifying land owners.

It is most unfortunate that the Senator is no economist and apparently is unaware of basic economic principles or laws that negate and subvert the kind of laws he would

[57]*Ibid.*, March 16, p. 36.
[58]*Ibid.*, p. 39.

impose. The coming food crisis he is describing in such vivid colors cannot be blamed on nature suddenly turning penurious and parsimonious, but only on man himself. It is explained by the economic law of shortage, which is applicable to all economic goods and services, including the means of subsistence. In simple formulation it reads as follows: *Wherever institutional restrictions stifle the creative energy of man, he lingers in want and shortage. In particular, when rampant inflation, confiscatory taxation and price controls destroy his productive division of labor, he is condemned to poverty. But where he is free from such restraints, he is enjoying the rich rewards of his labors and full cooperation of nature.* The energy crisis of recent years, which the Senator holds up as a warning, is merely another example of the inexorable working of this economic law.

We also doubt that $20 million tax relief, as provided by the Senator's bill, can alleviate "these confiscatory tax policies" and avert the coming collision. On the contrary, economic policies such as those prescribed by Senator Mathias, seeking to elevate political power over economic law, are fostering the very crisis they are said to prevent.

A grave crisis already has come into view in American education, especially private and parochial. With its insatiable hunger for revenue, government is forever searching for new tax opportunities in every corner and niche of economic life, including private education and health care, charitable foundations and organizations. In self-defense their representatives and councils are arguing their cases before the committees of Congress, pleading like defense attorneys whose clients are about to be sentenced. But while the private institutions of higher learning are appealing for tax mercy, it is rather quaint and bizarre that almost without exception their professors are the loudest proponents of higher tax levies.

The American Association of Presidents of Independent Colleges and Universities, the National Association of Independent Schools, the Christian and Missionary Alliance, together with many other institutions of higher learning, and the *National Association for Hospital Development,* all are opposing strenuously any proposals that would substantially reduce charitable gifts and bequests to such organizations. In particular, they are alarmed by proposals that would levy a tax on appreciation of property that is contributed to publicly supported charitable organizations or would place a 50 percent or other ceiling on the estate and gift tax charitable deductions.[59]

Their reasoning is clear and succinct although it suffers from the same narrow vision that is clouding many other pleas for mercy. While arguing for the uniqueness of their particular industries they arrive at almost identical recommendations: if Congress should decide to raise the estate and gift levies, it should not subject them to such levies. Unfortunately, they fail to explain why education and health care are so unique in public service and benefit, and why other industries, such as food, clothing and shelter that directly sustain human life, should be of lesser import than the industries serving health and education. But in spite of this self-serving speciosity their defense is a remarkable declaration of independence from political intervention. With survival at stake they are retreating to the solid foundation of moral and political principle:

> Charitable contributions by concerned citizens have enabled educational institutions to maintain freedom of academic inquiry. They have insured separation of church and state. Voluntary charitable contributions have offered the means of maintaining the historical balance between government services and voluntary initiatives, the antithesis of a totalitarian society. The charitable contribution deduction enables our citizens to participate in making decisions, rather than concentrating further power in the hands of the government. Reducing current tax incentives would reverse the objective of less, rather than more, government intervention.[60]

The *American Council on Education* represents virtually all of the accredited, public and private, nonprofit colleges and universities, as well as nonprofit elementary and secondary schools that enroll approximately ninety percent of the nation's private school children. Speaking for practically all institutions of learning serving some thirteen million students, it warns about the critical condition of schools, colleges and universities whose continued existence is at stake. New tax levies can only make matters worse. "We do

---

[59]*Ibid.*, March 19, p.38.
[60]*Ibid.*, pp. 42, 49.

not see how there could be resulting benefit or revenue to government. In short, we believe that the effect of the proposed changes with respect to gifts and bequests of property will not benefit the Treasury, but it will cause a substantial diminution of the support of public charities and in particular schools, colleges and universities at a time of dire financial stress."[61]

Unfortunately, this sagacious reasoning regarding cost and benefit of taxation is clouded by a blunt indifference toward basic principle: "We strongly urge that, if a tax on unrealized appreciation at death is imposed, there be an exception."[62]

The organizations of business testifying before the House Committee on Ways and Means usually argue from the vantage point of practical economic knowledge. At least they understand the importance of business capital, and know the effects of income taxes and capital levies on employment, wages, and profits. Having lived through the double-digit inflation of recent years they personally experienced the impact of inflation on prices and costs, on tax liabilities at progressive rates, and probably learned to distinguish illusory inflationary gains from real economic profits. It is refreshing to find so much rational economics in the statements of the leading business organizations. Unfortunately, in defense of the spiritual and moral antecedents of the private property order they are as frail and impotent as most other spokesmen for tax relief.

The *National Realty Committee* presents a sagacious analysis of the proposals that would increase death duties. But having first established that the industry is essentially a composite of "small entrepreneurial enterprises," and that estate and gift tax duties do not directly destroy small businesses, its statement to the Committee concludes that "sound tax policy mandates retention of the existing estate tax pattern ... While such an approach does not clearly facilitate capital formation, it at least has the limited virtue of administrative convenience and of not actively destroying small businesses and entrepreneurial real estate enter-

---

[61]*Ibid.*, p. 94.
[62]*Ibid.*, p. 95.

prises through forced sales required to pay both estate and income taxes."[63]

The *Council of Small Independent Business Associations* with a total membership of nearly 1 million business units makes a cogent case for a higher estate tax exemption, liberalization of stock redemptions to pay death taxes, and for lower tax rates for small business. Its rationale: inflation has eroded the exemptions and made the graduated structure of the tax too burdensome. But apparently this holds true only for "small businesses" with taxable estates of $1 million; for estates of over $1 million there must be "no change from present rates."[64]

The statement by the *Chamber of Commerce of the United States* reads like a summary of the position of other business organizations pleading for tax relief. It urges reduction in the estate and gift tax rates, an increase in the estate tax exemption, the gift lifetime exemption, and the gift tax annual exclusion. It opposes both the imposition of a tax on the value appreciation of capital assets at the time of transfer by death, and an additional tax on property transfers that skip one or more generations.

The Chamber even points at the deleterious effects of capital consumption and its consequences for the future:

Private capital is the basis of the American economic system, and a ready supply of such capital is essential to the stability and continued economic growth of the United States. According to the 1975 *Fortune* survey of industry medians of assets per employee, about $50,000 of capital is required on the average in a metal manufacturing business to employ one person. The federal estate and gift taxes are capital levies, and, as such, steadily reduced private capital available for investment. The result, but for inflation, can be a constant erosion of the tax base. If the estate tax deters the building of wealth through productive enterprise, there could come a time when comparatively little wealth would be available for capital ventures.[65]

Obviously, this perspicacious observation holds true not just for small capital holdings but especially for larger ones.

---

[63]*Ibid.*, March 15, p. 391.
[64]*Ibid.*, p. 437.
[65]*Ibid.*, p. 364.

95

The greater the capital consumption, the greater the erosion of productive capacity. But the Chamber does not draw this conclusion. Instead, in the next sentence it quickly returns to the mainstream of contemporary thought by pointing out that the estate tax problem can be particularly acute for small family-owned businesses.

The *National Association of Manufacturers* whose membership consists not only of thousands of small businessmen but also of some of the largest and wealthiest entrepreneurs in the country, is speaking especially softly before the committees of Congress. Lest it be accused of representing big business and great wealth, the favorite victims of estate and gift duties, it is pleading for its smallest members: "Because the fundamental problem of estate taxation is the *size* of the liability rather than the timing of payments, a general rate reduction is desirable, particularly in the steeply progressive brackets up to $100,000."[66] The Association even goes out of its way to plead the popular case of farmers who are not members of NAM. Small businesses and farmers should be granted a five-year, interest-free moratorium on payment of taxes, and annual payment over twenty years at a reduced interest rate of 4 percent. NAM admits that unification of the estate and gift tax structures might be desirable, but in view of the complications that would accompany it, the proposals should be studied and analyzed further. And how valiant is NAM's defense of its wealthy members, the primary victims of the trial? Visibly embarrassed, NAM is listening to the discussion and waiting docilely for the outcome.

The *New York Stock Exchange*, represented by its Chairman of the Board, James J. Needham, makes an interesting plea on behalf of the average farmer, small businessman, professional man and wage earner. The case is presented in the colorful garb of sociological considerations, and is directed at inflation that has shifted the burden of estate and gift taxation from the rich to the middle class:

> The Federal estate tax, if only because of inflation, has changed from a tax on the estates of the rich to a tax on the estates of the middle class. In the meantime, the very rich have solved most of their estate problems through such devices as trusts, *inter vivos* gifts, or other sophisticated

---

[66]*Ibid.*, March 16, p. 41.

maneuvers devised by able lawyers to outwit able legislators.

The net effect is that the average farmer, small businessman, professional, or wage earner who has worked hard all his life, made reasonably prudent investments and educated his family, but who has not had the foresight, inclination, or means to employ the nation's legal talent must now pay a disproportionate share of Federal estate tax revenue. The Federal estate tax system has led to a situation in which 1975 numbers are applied to 1942 dollars. I cannot believe that this Congress wishes these inequities to go on forever.[67]

Relying heavily on authoritative proof, e.g. Senator McGovern, and a group of experts at the Brookings Institution, Chairman Needham is pleading for readjustment of the tax burden to its original intent. After all, it is proper and fair "to reduce concentration of wealth perhaps once a generation with respect only to relatively large estates." This objective could be best achieved if the $60,000 exemption were increased to $200,000, which would exempt estates that in today's dollar value are small and medium-sized.

In contrast to this faint echo of a statement by the New York Stock Exchange the voice of the *Libertarian Advocate*, speaking through *Alan W. Bock*, is loud and clear. To the politicians in Congress who, in a sense of righteousness and omnipotence, now are spending more than $400 billion annually, all for the benefit of a greater society, it must be a voice that is shrill, rude, and belligerent. Mr. Bock must sound like a wild agitator: "The time has come to eliminate the inheritance tax and its cousin the gift tax from the arsenal of weapons which the federal government has evolved to harass its citizens." Obviously no one in the Congress, nor even in the sprawling administrative bureaucracy, sees himself as an "harasser" with an "arsenal of weapons" he has helped to build against the free society. And very few would admit that "the inheritance tax and its bastard cousin, the gift tax, are cruel taxes," in spite of the many excellent arguments Alan Bock raises against the levies.

The Libertarian statement even alienates its few listeners in the balcony when it presents its positive proposal:

---

[67]*Ibid.*, p. 50.

substitution of the federal income tax for inheritance and gift taxation. In Bock's own words:

Inheritances are not subject to income taxation. If inheritances and gifts were treated as income, with a liberalized provision for income averaging since it is unlikely that Congress will take the sensible step of eliminating the progressive feature of the income tax, the revenue could be made up easily, and much more equitably.[68]

If productive capital is taxed as income, even when averaged over several years, the tax burden obviously would multiply. A small inheritance would lift an heir from his 30 to 40 percent income tax bracket in which he may be now into the 50 percent bracket. And the heir to a multimillion dollar fortune would find himself condemned to the maximum bracket for the rest of his natural life. It would be neither economical nor equitable.

To most observers who are unaware of the existence of economic principles and inexorable laws, estate and gift taxes are ideal sources of federal revenue. They do not deter man's incentive to strive and work because they are paid when man by definition cannot take the money with him.[69] Of course, this is true for rich and poor alike, which denies any justification to the steep rate progression, since in death all men are equal. If society through its political institutions claims the right to appropriate the earthly belongings of the deceased it must claim it for all, young and old, rich and poor alike. To take possession of the material remains of its richer members only is to discriminate against them in favor of others. It creates inequality in death and conflict among the living.

Economists must seek beyond the banal observation that the dead cannot take it with them. In particular, they must inquire into the nature and function of the property which government would like to appropriate.

In a highly productive country, economic wealth consists almost exclusively of facilities of production. A government that proposes to tax or expropriate economic wealth is

---

[68]*Ibid.*, March 17, pp. 163, 164.
[69]Cf. Prof. David Westfall, *Background Materials on Federal Estate and Gift Taxation*, House Commiteee on Ways and Means, Committee Print, March 8, 1976, p. 104.

planning to consume such facilities employed in the production of goods and services for the people, giving them employment and livelihood. Taxes that consume this productive capital actually reduce labor productivity and wages and thus aggravate economic and social inequality. Progressive estate taxation, in particular, consumes productive capital and thus intensifies the inequality.

The statements and testimonies before the House Committee on Ways and Means provide an excellent sample of contemporary economic and social thought. The numerous spokesmen of special interests, arguing pro and con, are advising their legislators on how to divide properly and fairly the very substance of their economic existence. And not one economist is stepping forth, pointing at the inevitable consequences of capital consumption and the economic and social inequality it must engender.

A society that seeks equality by force is floundering in the darkness of economic ignorance and political pragmatism. In its search for economic equality through transfer programs it is moving from peace and prosperity to conflict and poverty.

CONCLUSION

The world is coming, more and more, to the belief that personal wealth is superfluous and evil and, therefore, should be seized and consumed for the common good. The leaders are preaching envy and resentment and promoting social conflict and strife. We must not permit extremes of wealth for a few, they warn us, together with enduring poverty for many. Society, acting through its political institutions, must alleviate the evil through redistribution of income and wealth.

Most policies of federal and state governments are built on these doctrines of poverty and wealth. With all means at its disposal the political apparatus is made to achieve more economic equality through spending, taxing, regulating, and a thousand other devices. But the more it is made to press for equality by force, the greater and more glaring the inequality tends to become. The desired objective of economic equality lies beyond the power of any government because it violates human nature and ignores the inborn inequalities of men. But even if all men were equal in talent, industry and thrift, they still would need to form productive capital in order to facilitate production and sustain their lives. They would need large concentrations of capital to achieve the levels of production that can sustain the teeming masses of mankind. And these concentrations would have to be applied unevenly to various economic pursuits. Heavy manufacturing requires more capital than service industries, which once again would lead to glaring inequalities in the use and possession of capital.

The dream of economic equality is a delusion and phantom of the mind. Any attempt to bring it about through political force is not only ineffective, but also harmful to economic well-being and social peace. It necessitates forever the use and application of force which, in the end, must give rise to a political, social and economic command system. It mandates the seizure of productive wealth which sustains human life, for the sake of present enjoyment at the expense of future production and consumption. It consumes productive capital, reduces economic production, lowers wage rates, and impoverishes those very individuals whom the policy is supposed to benefit.

Estate taxation is utterly unsuited to achieve the dream of equality. Born from envy and resentment, it fosters prodigality and dissipation and exasperates the poverty of the poor.

INDEX

A

accessions tax, 78
Adams, H.B., 32
aesthetics, 10
Ali, Muhammad, 8
American Association of Presidents of Independent Colleges and Universities, 92
American Bankers Association, 80,81,92
American Council on Education, 93
American Economic Association, 32
American Farm Bureau Federation, 53,88-89
American Forestry Association, 90
American Institute of Certified Public Accountants, 82-83
American Motors, 6
American National Cattlemen's Association, 90
Anderson, B. Ray, 76
annuity, 66-68
anthropology, 10
appreciation estate tax, 81
art objects, 20,39,61,76
A & P, 5
attorneys, 49,75
avoidance, 56-59

B

bankers, 22, 70-76
barbarism, 14
bearer instruments, 62
Bentham, Jeremy, 41-42
Bock, Alan W., 97-98
bond market, 71
bonds, 74
bonus, 7
Brannon, G. M., 86-87
Brookings Institution, 86,97
Buchanan, James M., 24
Burke, Edmund, 37
business cycles, 15
businessmen, 22, 67-68

C

California, 47
capitalism, 3,87
Carnegie, Andrew, 34
Carter, Jimmy, 36
certificates, 74
Chamber of Commerce of the United States, 95
charitable deductions, 93
charitable giving, 57-58
charitable institution, 22,71
China, 4
Christian and Missionary Alliance, 92
Chrysler Corp., 4
Chrysler, Walter P., 7
Civil War, 14,29
Clark, J. M., 34
collectors, 20
colleges, 22,71
colonists, 13
command system, 2,52
commercial paper, 62
Committee on Ways and Means, 77, 84,94,98-99
Commons, J. R., 34
common stock, 68,73
competition, 8,18,52
Comptroller of the Currency, 74
Connecticut, 54
Constitution, U.S., 13,77
corporations, 68
Council of Small Independent Business Association, 95
courts, 73

D

debentures, 21
Debs, E.V., 34
debt, 26-27
debt liquidation, 21
defense spending, 16
Democratic Party, 34,87
depressions, 14-15,35, 53
development rights, 85-86
diamonds, 61,76
Dietze, Gottfried, 39
direct taxes, 13
Dow Jones averages, 72

E

economists, 9-10,98
Economic Recovery Tax Act, 20, 30-31,51,56,75,80-81
education, 92-94
elderly, 16
Ely, R. T., 32
energy crisis, 92
England, 1-2,35
English Classical School, 32
equality, 11-12,17,18,37-40
estate taxation, 19
ethics, 10
evasion, 59-61
excess income, 18

exclusion, 56
executives, 7-8

F
family annuity, 66
farms, 53-55,67-68
Federalists, 29
Federal Reserve Board, 74
Federal Reserve System, 15
financiers, 22
Florida, 44-47
Ford Corporation, 6
Ford, Gerald, 86
Ford, Henry, 4,48,59
Forest Industries Committee, 90
Fortune, 95
foundations, 58-59,78
Franklin, Benjamin, 43
Friedman, Rose D., 11

G
General Motors Corporation, 4,46
general partners, 67-68
generation-skipping transfers, 84-85
George, Henry, 31
German Historical School, 32
gift taxes, 18-19
gold, 61-76
Graetz, M. J., 86
Grant, Allan, 88-89

H
Halbach, E. C., 86
Haney, L. H., 33
Harris, 78
Hawaii, 47
Hayek, F. A., 17
Hazlitt, Henry, 11
history, federal estate taxes, 28-36
holding companies, 68
Hoover, Herbert Clark, 26,35-36
humanism, 20

I
Idaho, 54
immorality, 17
import duties, 13
income security, 12
Income Tax Act of 1894, 30
income tax, corporate, 24
India, 4
Indiana, 54
industrial bonds, 62
inequality, 3-12,18-19
inflation, 15,21-27,64-69
inheritance tax, 29,78

Institute of Certified Public
  Accountants, 82
Institutionalists, 33
interest, 5
Internal Revenue Service, 54
investors, 22
invisible wealth, 61
Iowa, 54
Iron Curtain countries, 60

J
Jantscher, G. R., 86
Jefferson, Thomas, 29
jewelry, 20,39,61
Johnson, Lyndon B., 10
joie de vivre, 45

K
Kennedy, Edward M., 83-86
Keynesianism, 15

L
LaFollette, R. M., 34
Lane, Laura, 51
law of cost, 23
legislators, 18
Libertarian Advocate, 97
life insurance, 21,66,67
limited partnership, 67-68
literary foundations, 22,71
loopholes, 19,59,78,79-87,89,91
luxuries, 46,47

M
Madison, James, 14
Maine, 54
management, 7
managerial remuneration, 5
Marshall, Justice, 37
Mathias, Charles C., 90-92
Marx, Karl, 33,34,87
Maryland Historical Trust, 90
Maxwell-Chalmers Corp., 7
McGovern, G., 97
Medicaid, 16
medical expenses, 56
Medicare, 16
Midcontinent Farmers
  Association, 90
military, U.S., 16
millionaires, 54
Minnesota, 54
minorities, 13
Mises, Ludwig von, 38
Mitchell, W. C., 34
Montana, 54
morality, 19
municipals, 62

N

National Association for Hospital
 Development, 92
National Association of Independent
 Schools, 92
National Association of Manufacturers, 96
National Association of Wheat Growers,
 90
National Centers for Health Statistics, 50
National Farmers Union, 90
National Live Stock Committee, 90
National Realty Committee, 94
National Register of Historic Places, 90
Nebraska, 54
Needham, James J., 96-97
Nevada, 28
New Deal, 34
New Jersey, 54
New York, 54
New York Stock Exchange, 96-97
New York Times, 54
Normans, 1
North Dakota, 54
North, Gary, 63
nouveaux riches, 25-27
nuclear war, 14

O

old age pensions, 17
options, 8
Opitz, Edmund A., 39

P

paintings, 61
partition, 41-42
Patten, S. N., 32
Pechman, J. A., 52,78
pension funds, 21
philanthropy, 50
Pigou, A. C., 42
Plains Cotton Growers, Inc., 90
political parties, 9
politicians, 73
politics, 10
poverty, 9-11,100
precious metals, 20,39,61
predecessors, 41-47
preferred stock, 68, 73
premium, 62
Prentice, E. P., 39
pressure groups, 13
prices, 22-24
primitive history, 2
private property, 1-12
privilege, 4,9
probate, 76
professional corporation, 57

profit, 4-7
Progressive Party, 35
property rights, 2
prudent-man rule, 73
psychology, 10
Public Citizen Tax Reform
 Research Group, 82
public opinion, 9,77
public services, 16,17

R

rajah, 4
ranching, 67-68
Read, Leonard E., 39
real estate, 72
recapture taxes, 61,67
redistribution, 16,21,25
reformers, 9,77
reform proposals, 77-99
religious societies, 22,71
Republican Party, 34,87
rentiers, 22
revocable living trusts, 70,75
Rockefeller, John D., 48,59
Roosevelt, Franklin D., 10,34,36
Roosevelt, Theodore, 35
Rushdoony, R. J., 20

S

Sager, William S., 28
scientific foundations, 22,71
Seligman, E.R.A., 32
Sennholz, H. F., 22,24
shortages, 90-92
Shoup, C. A., 86
Shultz, William J., 29,30,78
silver, 76
Simon, William E., 79-82
Sinatra, Frank, 8
Sixteenth Amendment, 13,35
slaves, 13
Slichter, S. H., 34
small business, 51-53
Smith, J., 86
social classes, 18
Socialist Party, 34
sociology, 10
Soviet Union, 60
Spanish-American War, 30
speculators, 21,91
stamp tax, 29
Standard & Poor's 500, 72
starvation, 91
steelworkers, 25
stepped-up annuities, 66
stock, 8,21,71-72
stock brokers, 22

student loans, 16
Subchapter S, 76
successors, 48-55
Sumner, William Graham, 31
Swiss banks, 28,39,60
Switzerland, 28

T
Taft, William Howard, 35
Taxation with Representation, 83
Tax Equity and Fiscal Responsibility Act, 62,75
tax progression, 17,23,37
Tax Reform Act, 30,51,56,81,83,89
tax reforms, 15
Taylor, Elizabeth, 8
Third-World countries, 60
Thomas, Norman, 34
time deposits, 21
trust companies, 71
trusts, 70-76
tuition, 56

U
Ullman, Al, 84
underground economy, 20,60

unearned income, 64
U.S. Steel Corp., 8
U.S. Treasury, 15,46,53,65
U.S. Trust Co., 54
universities, 22,71
use valuation, 61

V
Value Line Index, 72
vassals, 13
Veblen, Thorstein, 33
voting preferred stock, 68

W
Walker, Amasa, 31
Walker, Francia A., 31
war, 14
Westfall, D., 98
widow tax, 50,80
William the Conquerer, 1-2
Wilson, Woodrow, 35
Wisconsin, 34,54
women's liberation movement, 50
World War I, 14
World War II, 14